Building the HANS Electric Gear Clock

The Illustrated Guide to Building an Heirloom Electric Gear Clock

Michael Simpson

Kronos Robotics
July 2012

Building the HANS Electric Gear Clock
Published by Kronos Robotics
Leesburg, Virginia

All rights reserved.
Copyright © 2012 by Michael G Simpson

No part of this book may be reproduced or transmitted in any form or by any means, electronic or mechanical, including photocopying, recording, or by any information storage and retrieval system, without permission in writing from the publisher.

The publisher (Kronos Robotics) grants the purchaser of this book the right to make copies of Appendix A in order to re size the drawings as needed. These copies should be used for personal use only.

ISBN 978-1-938687-01-3

Dedicated to my new granddaughter, JANE WINREY, and her mother and father, ISABEL AND JACK.

Forward

HANS is a wooden gear clock that was designed from the ground up to help you successfully build your first gear clock. Many wooden gear clocks utilize weights to power the gear clock. These weights mean you have to wind the clock ever couple days. The HANS electric gear clock utilizes an easy to obtain synchronous motor to drive the clock. This motor attached to the first gear, will keep the clock accurate to within a second or two each month.

Table of Contents

Getting Started 1
Cutting the Gears 7
Clock Spacers 23
Gear Assembly 33
Clock Face and Hands 45
Clock Plates 53
Front Plate Assembly 73
Final Assembly 81
Finishing The Clock 99
Conclusion 111
Drawings 113

!! IMPORTANT !!
Please Read

You will need these files in order to complete some of the chapters in this book. The files can be found here:

http://www.kronosrobotics.com/hans/dz19781_9386_87013/

In addition you can find much more information about HANS here:

http://www.kronosrobotics.com/hans/

Chapter 1

Getting Started

W hat is the HANS electric gear clock? HANS is a wooden gear clock that was designed from the ground up to help you successfully build your first gear clock.

This book will take you step by step through the process of building a real working gear clock. Throughout the process, you will be given opportunity to make basic changes that will effect the personality of your creation.

While the design of the clock had beginners in mind, there are still certain tools you will need to build this clock.

Gear Creation

The wooden gears used by HANS are not only the key component to this clock, they are also the most difficult component. There are three methods that can be used to obtain the wooden gears.

- Creating the gears by using the scroll saw method
- Creating the gears by using the router table method
- Purchase the gears

Scroll Saw Method

This method involves attaching a full size drawing to the stock and cutting each tooth individually. Once the teeth are cut, a small hole is drilled inside the waste area of the spoke. The blade of the scroll saw is then inserted into the hole and attached to the saw, and the waste is cut out of the spoke. This process is repeated for each spoke.

Please note that a band saw may also be used to cut the teeth; however a band saw cannot be used to cut the spokes as there is no way to pass the blade into the waste area.

The scroll saw method is a very time-consuming method. One small mistake and the gear can be ruined. You must be a skilled scroll saw operator to use this method. For more information on this method see Chapter 2, "Cutting the Gears".

Router Table Method

This method requires the use of templates and a pin router attachment. The templates are available on the Kronos Robotics web site. The pin router attachment, like the one shown in Figure 1.1, can be purchased for under $50 online.

With the templates and pin router attachment, you will be able to quickly and accurately cut the gears. For more information on this method see Chapter 2, "Cutting the Gears".

Figure 1.1

Purchase The Gears

It's possible you don't have a router table, or you just don't want to cut the gears yourself. For this reason, a complete set of gears for the HANS clock are available on the Kronos Robotics web site.

Tools Needed to Build HANS

Aside from the tools needed for cutting the gears, there are additional tools needed for boring holes, cutting plates, and assembling the clock. The following are a list of those tools.

Drill Press

You absolutely must have a drill press to build clocks. Without a drill press there is no way to create arbor holes that are square enough for a clock to run accurately. The drill press used does not have to be a large expensive drill press. A small 10" drill press can be purchased for about $100. This will work just fine.

Drill Bits

You will need the following drill bit types and sizes:

1/8", 3/16", 7/32", 15/64", 1/4", 9/32", 7/16" Drill bits

5/8", 2" Forstner bits

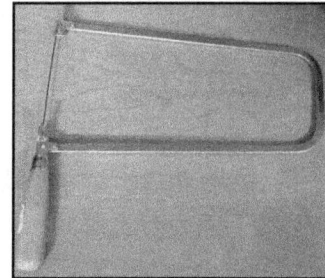
Figure 1.2

Scroll Saw

A scroll saw is needed if you are going to use the scroll saw method to cut your gears. If not, then it becomes an optional tool. For instance, depending on the design you choose, you will need to cut out a larger circular hole in the front plate. This can be cut easily with a scroll saw. It can also be cut quite effectively with a jig saw.

The clock hands and thin spacers also need to be cut with a scroll saw. They can also be cut by hand with a jewelers saw like the one shown in Figure 1.2.

Router Table

A router table is needed if you are going to use the pin router method to cut your gears; however a router table can also be used to round over the edges of your gears and plates. While rounding the edges is optional, it can give your clock a finished look.

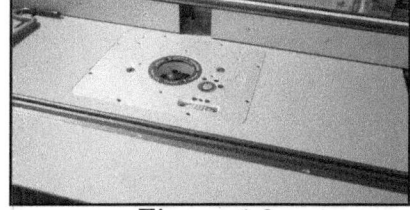
Figure 1.3

The router table can be an elaborate table like the one shown in Figure 1.3, or can be as simple as the router mounted under a piece of 3/4" MDF.

Note that you can use a small hand held router to round over the edges of the larger gears and plates. You will need the following bits for your router table:

1/8" Round over bit

1/8" Spiral bit. (Only needed if using router table to cut gears)

Other Tools

The following tools will be used at various times in the building process: Tubing cutter, wire cutters, razor knife, wooden mallet, Phillips screwdriver, layout tools, dial calipers, cordless power drill, center punch.

Electric Motor

HANS utilizes the 1 RPM Synchron motor shown in Figure 1.1. These can be purchased from Timesavers at www.timesavers.com, part number 18404.

There are other synchronous motors that may be used as well. Many of these can be purchased from eBay. If they are attached to the first gear you need to make sure they are 1 RPM motors. Many of these older motors come in a pear shaped design. The plate layout drawings include a cutout to accommodate the shape.

Figure 1.1

Materials

You can use a great many materials to build HANS. It is recommended however, that you build your first clock using 1/2" MDF. MDF is cheap and easy to work with. It finishes up very nicely when painted. All the clocks shown in this book were created using MDF. Once you build a clock or two you can switch to other materials.

For the clock plates you can use any material. Hardwoods like Cherry and Walnut make very nice plates, faces, and clock hands. When using hardwood on clock hands, make sure the grain runs the length of the hand.

The gears should not be made from solid wood as the gear teeth will chip off. If you want to use hard wood, you will have to glue up thin sheets of 1/8" stock, rotating the grain, to build up 1/2" stock. You can also use Baltic birch plywood or other species of 1/2" cabinet grade plywood.

The thin spacers should all be made from 1/8" hardboard. These can be cut with a scroll saw or jewelers saw, or, can be purchased from the Kronos Robotics web site,

Brass Tubing

Brass tubing is used to form the arbors in HANS. Figure 1.2 shows the three sizes used to build HANS, 7/32", 1/4" and 9/32". You will need about 12" lengths of each size. Most hobby shops sell brass tubing in 12" and 36" lengths. If you plan on building more than one clock, it may be worth it to purchase the longer lengths.

Brass tubing is manufactured so that each increment will fit inside the previous. For instance a 7/32" tube will fit inside a 1/4" tube, and 1/4" tube will fit inside a 9/32" tube.

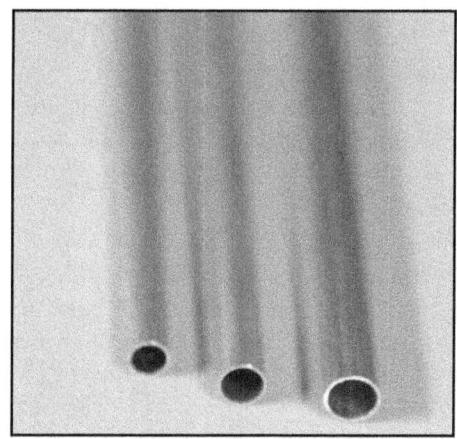

Figure 1.2

Cutting Brass Tubing

An easy way to cut brass tubing is with a tubing cutter like the ones shown in Figure 1.3.

For the sizes need in this project, the smaller cutter will work the best. You can purchases tubing cutters in the plumbing section of most home centers or hardware stores.

Do a search online and you can purchase the small cutter for less than $10.

If you are going to be building a lot of clocks then you might want to consider a small electric cutoff saw like the one shown in Figure 1.4.

These saws make short work of cutting brass tubing. Once cut, the tubing requires less cleanup.

The can be found online for under $50.

Figure 1.3

Figure 1.4

Cleaning Tubing Cuts

Cutting brass tubing with a tubing cutter will bevel the inside edge of the tubing. This will need to be cleaned up before using the tubing. The tubing reamer shown in Figure 1.5 can help with the cleaning process.

Because the tubing used in this project is so small, a file and razor knife like the ones shown in Figure 1.6 will probably work the best. Brass is a very soft metal and the razor knife can cut small slivers off the inside or outside edges of the tubing.

Figure 1.5

Brass Tube Assembly

During the assembly process, you will be told the type tubing to use and its lengths. It is best to cut the tubing as you progress through the project.

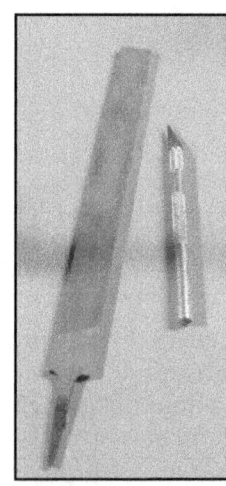

Figure 1.6

Before Starting

Be sure to visit the Kronos Robotics web site for updates, tips and other useful information that will help you through building process.

If you own or have access to a laser or CNC machine, Kronos Robotics sells a DVD with drawing files that can be used to create most of the parts used to build the clock.

Information more information on HANS and available parts visit the Kronos Robotics web site:

http://www.kronosrobotics.com/hans/

Chapter 2

Cutting the Gears

The gears are the most important components in a wooden gear clock. If they are not cut correctly the clock will not run. HANS was designed for simplicity and utilizes eight gears to deliver power to the hour and minute hands.

Even though HANS is a simple clock to build, cutting the eight gears represent the bulk of the effort in building this clock.

Tools Needed For This Chapter

- Scroll saw, band saw, or router table (see text)
- Router table with pin router attachment (see text)
- 1/8" Round over bit
- Drill press
- 1/4" Drill bit
- 1/8" Drill bit
- 9/32" Drill bit
- 3/16" Drill bit
- 5/8" Forstner bit

Components Needed For This Chapter

- 1, 8" x 8" piece of 1/2" MDF
- 1, 8-1/2" x 8-1/2" Piece of 1/2" MDF
- 1, 5-1/2" x 5-1/2" Piece of 1/2" MDF
- 1, 6-1/2" x 6-1/2" Piece of 1/2" MDF
- 1, 6" x 6" Piece of 1/2" MDF
- Set of Kronos Robotics gear templates #GS1H (see text)
- 35, #6 x 1" Machine screws (see text)

Prerequisites

The HANS electric gear clock can be built from a single piece of 24" x 48" x 1/2" MDF. For this chapter you will need the following pieces cut in order using either the scroll saw or router method to cut the gears.

1, 8" x 8" piece

1, 8-1/2" x 8-1/2" piece

1, 5-1/2" x 5-1/2" piece

1, 6" x 6" piece

1, 6-1/2" x 6-1/2" piece

Appendix A contains a set of drawings that may be copied to provide templates for cutting the gears with a scroll saw.

If you are going to use a router table, you will need a set of gear templates and pin router attachment for your router table. In addition, you will need 35, #6 x 1" machine screws. It is important that the machine screw not protrude all the way through the template or you may scratch your table. A small #6 washer will solve this problem. If you are not using 1/2" MDF as your stock material, you may want to use smaller screws.

If you don't own a pin router attachment for your router table you can purchase one from MCLS #1221 for under $50. The templates used to make the HANS gears can be purchased from the Kronos Robotics web site, part number GS1H.

As an option, Kronos Robotics also offers a set of 1/2" MDF gears like the ones shown in Figure 2.1. These are great for first time clock builders. The part number for this set is HANSGS1.

Figure 2.1

Building the Hans Electric Gear Clock

Gear cutting can be extremely time consuming and with the larger gears very frustrating. It is important that you use a method that is best suited to your skills and tools. For instance, if you own and are skilled at using a scroll saw then that is probably the best route to take. If you own a router table, you may prefer using that method.

Cutting with a Scroll Saw or Band Saw

Cutting gears with a scroll saw or band saw requires great attention to detail. It is probably the most time consuming method of cutting wooden gears. If you are not reasonably skilled at operating a scroll saw, it is recommended that you use a router table to cut your gears.

You can also use a band saw to cut the wooden gears. The set up and cutting technique described below is identical for both saws, with the exception that you cannot make the internal spoke cutouts with a band saw.

Step 1 - Prepare the Template

You will need full size cutouts of the gears in order to use a scroll or band saw. Appendix A has a set of drawings that can be copied on a copy machine and resized. Figure 2.2 shows an example of the gear 9 drawing. It is important that you enlarge the gear so that its final size is that which is indicated in the drawing. For instance gear 9 is reduced 80%. It must be enlarged 125% in order that the final size of 6" x 6" is achieved. After enlarging the template, measure the dimensions. Even slight changes in scale may result in a clock that does not work.

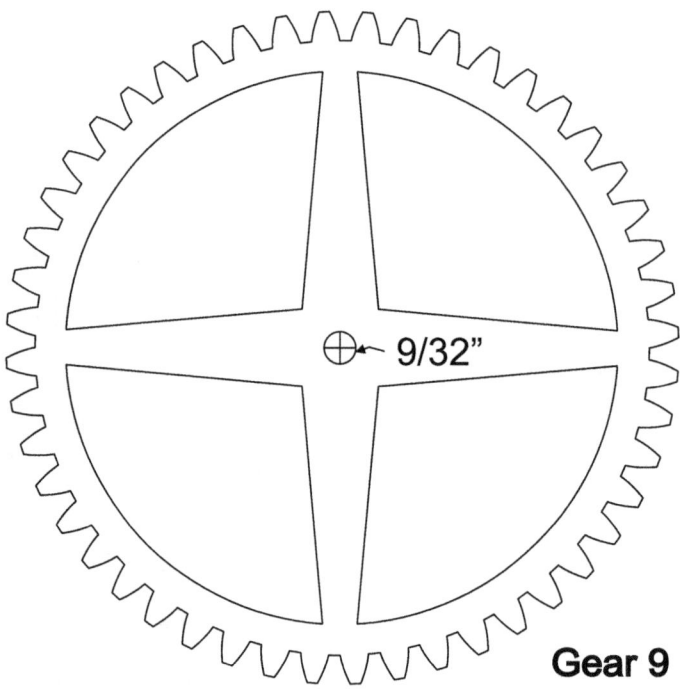

Figure 2.2

Step 2 - Attach the Template

The template needs to be attached to the material you are making your gears out of. You can use double sided tape, as shown in Figure 2.3, or you can use spray adhesive.

Step 3 - Drill the Center Hole

All the gear drawings have markings showing the location and size of the hole to be made in each gear. This must be drilled with a drill press. Failure to use a drill press could result in a hole that is not exactly perpendicular to the gear.

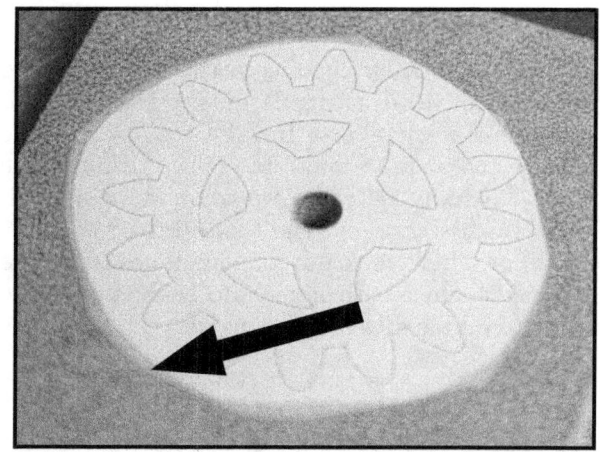

Figure 2.3

Tip

Use a center punch to dent the center of the gear before drilling. This will ensure the hole will be dead center.

Step 4 - Rough Cut the Gear

Cut along the tip of the teeth in order to cut the base shape of the gear out, as shown in Figure 2.4. This will make cutting the teeth much simpler.

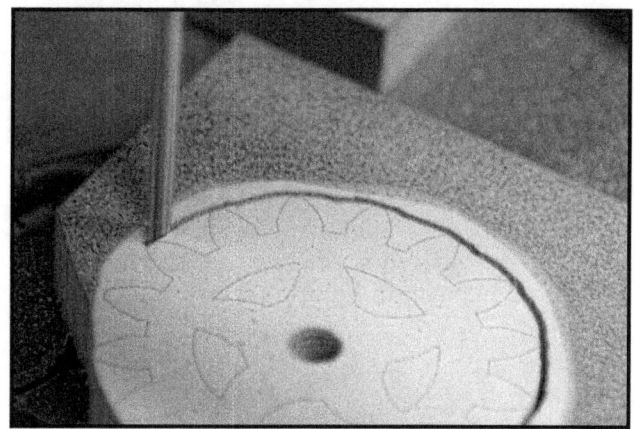

Figure 2.4

Building the Hans Electric Gear Clock

Step 5 - Cut the Teeth

Cut the teeth by cutting in the middle of the tooth line of the drawing. If you are using a band saw like the one shown in Figure 2.5, the blade may be too wide to make the curve through the fillet. This may be true even when using a scroll saw. In this case, cut the tooth until you reach the fillet, then back out the blade and cut the other side. Once both sides have been cut use the blade to nibble away at the inside.

Step 6 - Cut the Spokes

The larger gears have spokes. To cut the spokes, use a 1/4" drill bit to make a hole through the waste area of all the spokes. You can only cut out the spokes if you are using a scroll saw.

Detach the blade from the saw and slip it through the hole. With the blade inserted through the hole reattach to the saw.

Cut the waste area out and repeat on the next spoke.

Figure 2.5

Cutting With a Router Table

The easiest and most accurate way to cut the gears is by using a router table. In order to use a router table you will need a pin router attachment like the one shown in Figure 2.6.

Figure 2.6

12   *Chapter 2*   Cutting the Gears

The pin router attachment is used with a set of templates like the ones shown in Figure 2.7. Each template is first attached to the stock with screws or double sided tape. The pin router attachment is then used to guide the template and stock over the router bit in the router table.

Figure 2.7

Step 1 - Tape Stock to Template

Your stock should be cut to the same size as the template. For example, the gear 3 template is 8" x 8". The stock for this template should be 8" x 8".

Place the stock against the bottom of the template and tape it in place with some masking tape, as shown in Figure 2.8.

Tape all four corners.

Figure 2.8

Step 2 - Drill Four Corners

Use a drill press with 1/8" drill bit to make the four pilot holes on the corners, as shown in Figure 2.9. Drill all the way through the stock.

Make sure you use a piece of scrap under the stock or you may blow out the bottom of the hole.

When drilling, be sure to drill only a 1/4" or so at a time, pulling the bit out to clear the debris.

Figure 2.9

Step 3 - Attach Screws

Attach a #6 x 1" machine screw through the template and into the stock, as shown in Figure 2.10. Make sure the screw is not sticking out the bottom of the stock or it may scratch your router table. If it is, remove the screw and attach a #6 washer.

Note that if you do have to use a washer, then you should include washers on all the screws from this point on.

Remove the masking tape.

Figure 2.10

Step 4 - Drill and Install Remaining Screws

Using a 1/8" drill bit and drill press, drill all the remaining holes. Attach the #6 screws to all the holes.

Note that the larger gears don't need screws in the 5 center holes, as shown in Figure 2.11.

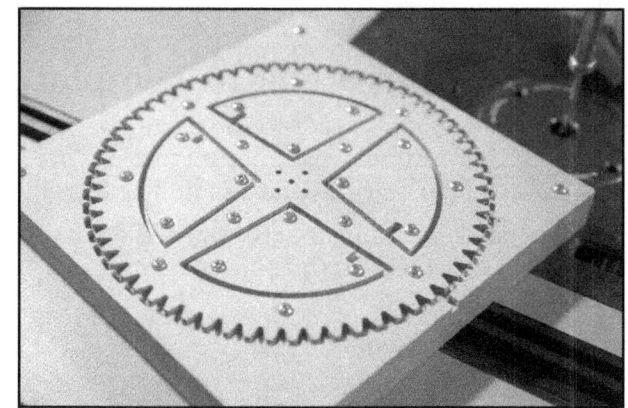

Figure 2.11

Step 5 - Align Pin Router

Place a 1/8" router bit in your router table and attach the 1/8" pin on the pin router attachment.

Align the tip with the bit and tighten the attachment. Raise the bit to 1/8" above the table, as shown in Figure 2.12.

The easiest way to align the pin with the bit is to take a piece of scrap and drill a 1/8" hole all the way through. From the underside of the scrap, place the hole over the bit. Next, lower the pin into the hole on the upper side of the scrap. Tighten the pin knob and all the mounting nuts on your pin router.

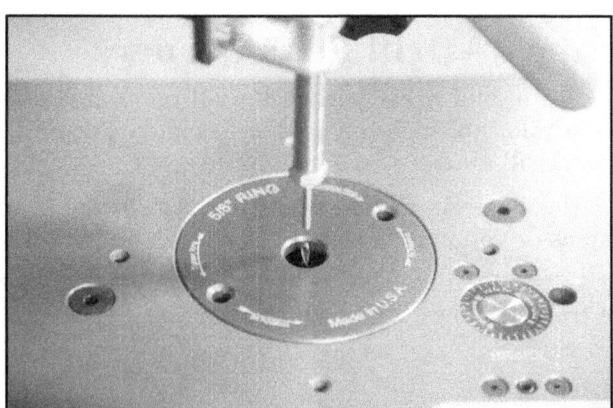

Figure 2.12

Step 6 - Cut the Teeth

Lower the pin so that it will fit into the grove of the template, as shown in Figure 2.13A. Turn the router on and slowly push the template/stock assembly into the pin via the entry slot, as shown in Figure 2.13B.

You want to push the teeth on the template against the pin and work your way around the gear rotating it counter clockwise.

Once you make one complete revolution, back the gear out through the entry slot. As you are cutting the teeth it is important to always keep both hands on the template. Don't cut too fast.

Once the pin has been removed, turn off the router and raise the bit another 1/8" and complete the process again.

In 1/2" stock you will need to make 4 passes to cut completely through. Start with 1/8", then 1/4" then 3/8" and finally just a smudge over 1/2" to make sure you cut through the stock.

Once you cut the teeth all the way through, Lower the bit back down to 1/8" above the table.

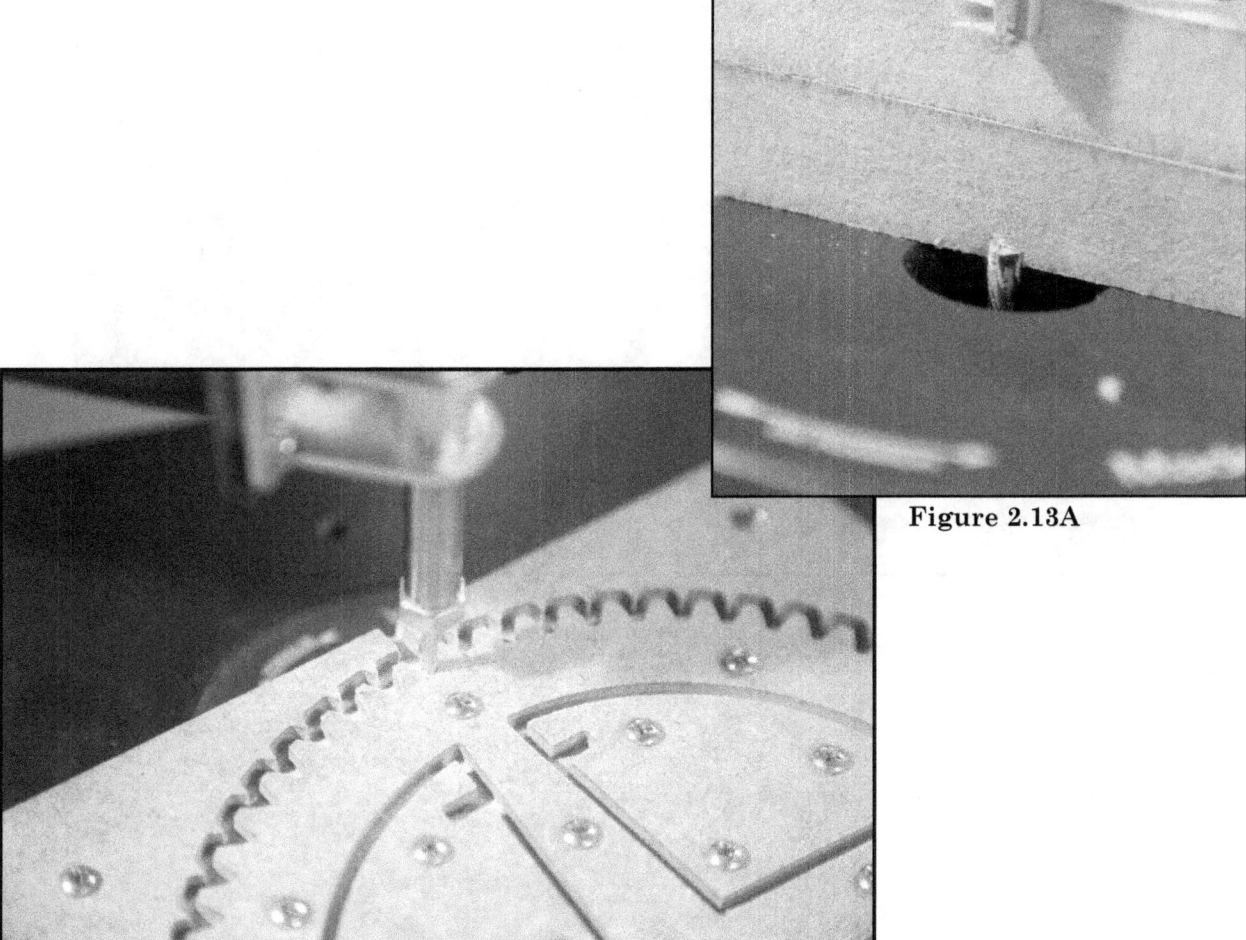

Figure 2.13A

Figure 2.13B

Step 7 - Inside Cuts

To make an inside cut with the pin router and a template, turn off the router. Raise the pin well above the template with the lever. Hold the template/stock assembly above the bit with the pin setting in the landing pad, as shown in Figure 2.14.

While still holding the template/stock above the bit, turn the router on. Holding the template against the pin use the lever to press the template/stock against the table. Once the stock is against the table, tighten the pin knob.

The key here is to keep the pin in that landing area as you lower the stock against the bit.

Figure 2.14

Tip

Always tighten the pin knob before cutting for the most accurate cut.

Proceed cutting around the inside grove, keeping the pin against the spoke, as shown in Figure 2.15. Once you have made a complete revolution move the pin back into the landing area and shut the router down.

DO NOT LIFT THE TEMPLATE UNTIL THE ROUTER HAS COME TO A COMPLETE STOP!!

Once the router has stopped loosen the pin knob and raise the pin above the template. Remove the template and adjust the router bit to the next level and repeat the process. Do this until you have made all four passes, then lower the bit to 1/8" and move to the next inside cut.

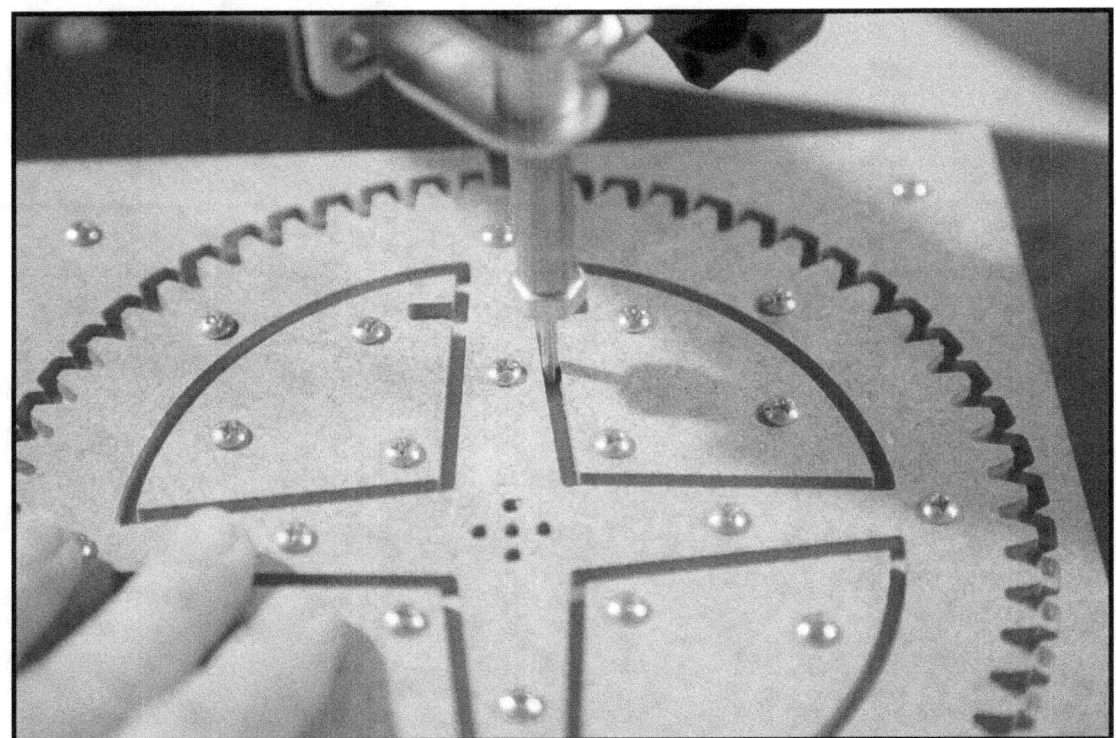

Figure 2.15

Tip
Visit the Kronos Robotics web site for video links showing the complete process for cutting gears.

Step 8 - Remove the Gear

Remove all the screws, as shown in Figure 2.16. Your finished gear should look like the gear shown in Figure 2.17

Figure 2.16

Figure 2.17

Step 9 - Cut the Remaining Gears

Repeat the process using all the templates to cut the eight gears and three spacers shown in Figure 2.18

Figure 2.18

Tip

You can also use double sided tape to attach your stock to the template. Don't use reenforced carpet tape as it is almost impossible to remove. The cheap paper backed carpet tape found at department stores works very well. Test it on some scrap first.

To use, apply strips to the stock, as shown in Figure 2.19, then place the template on top, aligning the edges.

Note that when using double stick tape, you still need to drill the center hole.

Figure 2.19

Finishing the Gears

This portion of the gear cutting process is completely optional, but it will give your gears a more formed look. The milled edge will also keep the gears from chipping later.

It is not recommended to mill the two smaller gears and spacers as they are too small to safely hold onto.

Step 1 - Install 1/8" Round Over Bit

Insert a 1/8" round over bit into the table and set it so that it takes a slightly less than 1/8" bite out of a piece of scrap, as shown in Figure 2.20.

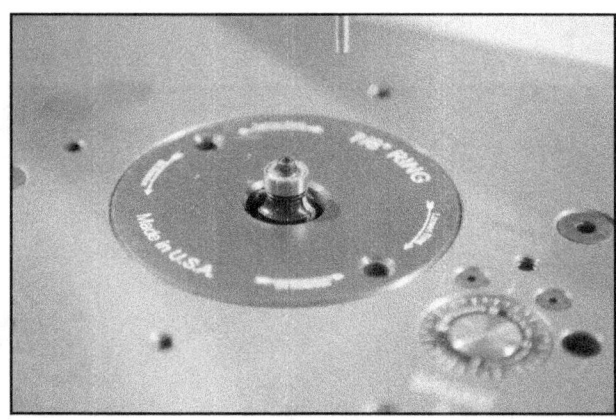

Figure 2.20

Step 2 - Round Over Inside Cuts

Mill the edge of the inside cuts, as shown in Figure 2.21.

Figure 2.21

Step 3 - Round Over Teeth

Mill the edge of the teeth, as shown in Figure 2.21.

Milling the teeth well help keep some laminated materials from chipping over time.

Figure 2.21

The completed set of gears should look like the ones shown here in Figure 2.22.

Figure 2.22

Step 4 - Drill the Gear Centers

Using a drill press, enlarge the pilot holes using the following chart.

Gear Number	Center Hole Diameter
3	1/4"
4	1/4"
5	1/4"
6	1/4"
7	9/32"
8	9/32"
9	9/32"
Drive gear	3/16"

Figure 2.23

Do not use a brad point bit. Let the shape of the bit auto center on the pilot hole as you drill. You must use a drill press to drill these holes, as shown in Figure 2.23.

Gear 7 has a 5/8" pocket that is .17" deep, as shown in Figure 2.24. This pocket is used to allow a locking washer to hold the gear in place. The washer is 1/2" in diameter and .125" thick. As long as the pocket is a little larger than the washer, it will fit.

Note that you can always enlarge the pocket at a later time if needed.

Figure 2.24

Conclusion

The HANS clock gears are now complete. They should look like the gears shown in Figure 2.25. If you cut the gears with a scroll or band saw they won't have the additional holes.

If you did use the templates and don't want the holes to show, you can fill them in with a little wood putty and sand them smooth. You can also add some small #6 x 1/4" brass screws to the holes in the spokes and rim of the gear. While the screws won't really do anything, they will look cool.

If you do decide to use the screws, you will want to counter sink the hole slightly so the heads are flush with the surface.

Figure 2.25

Chapter 3

Clock Spacers

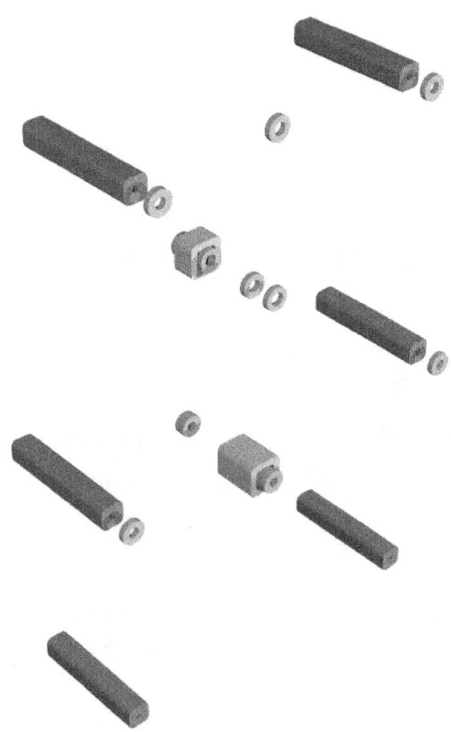

S pacers are used to align the clock gears. They are also used to hold the front and rear clock plates together.

While they are not critical components in the clock, it is important that they be made as close to the specified dimensions as possible.

Tools Needed For This Chapter

- Scroll or Band saw (used to cut some of the spacers)
- Drill press
- 1/8" Drill bit
- 1/4" Drill bit
- 7/32" Drill bit
- 9/32" Drill bit
- 15/64" Drill bit

Components Needed For This Chapter

- 1, 3" x 4" piece of 1/2" stock used to make the plate spacers
- 1, 4" x 4" piece of 1/2" stock used to make the thick spacers
- 2, 6" x 6" pieces of 1/8" stock used to make the thin spacers
- 1, 6" x 6" piece of 1/8" stock used to make the gear spacers

The sizes for the spacers shown here are based on the template drawings in Appendix A. If you cut them out of different sized material, copy and size the drawings, then cut out each piece and use it as needed.

Prerequisites

There are no prerequisites to cutting the spacers. They do need to be completed by the time you start the gear assembly.

The plate spacers should be made from the same stock as the front and rear plates. The thick spacers should be cut from the same stock that the gears are made of.

The gear spacers and thin spacers should be made from hardboard. You could also make them out of 1/8" or 3mm baltic birch.

There are four different types of spacers used in the HANS electric gear clock. The various types are shown in Figure 3.1.

Drawings are provided in Appendix A for each type of spacer. Please refer to these drawings in addition to the drawings presented here to help clarify construction of the spacers.

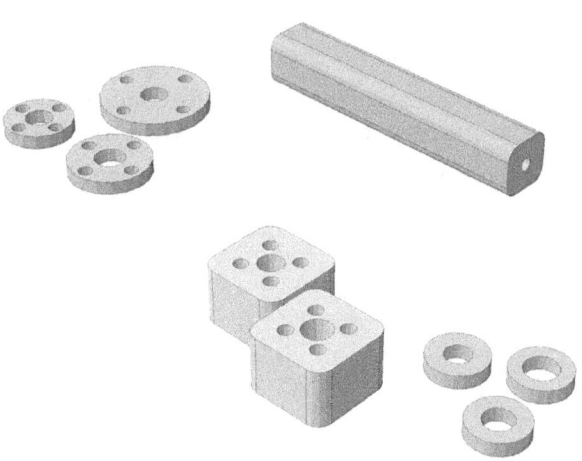

Figure 3.1

Clock Plate Spacers

Plate spacers like the one shown in Figure 3.2 are used to hold the front and rear clock plates together.

The plate spacers are 2-3/4" long and have a 1/8" pilot hole in each end. The pilot needs to be at least 1" deep.

The plate spacers can be made from any material.

The actual thickness of the material will dictate the thickness. For instance, if you are using MDF, a 3/4" thick spacer will be less likely to split then a 1/2" thick spacer.

You will need six plate spacers. It is recommended that the material for the plate spacer be the same as the front and rear plates.

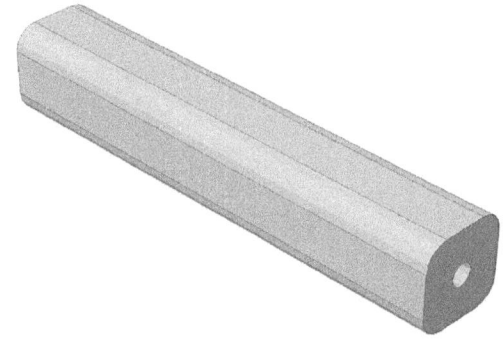

Figure 3.2

Figure 3.3 shows a detailed drawing of the plate spacers. The drawing shows the 1/8" pilot hole extending the full length of the spacer. You must use a drill press to drill this hole. Drill through half the length of the hole from each end of the plate spacer.

It is recommended that you use a 1/8" round over bit to fillet the edges of the spacer.

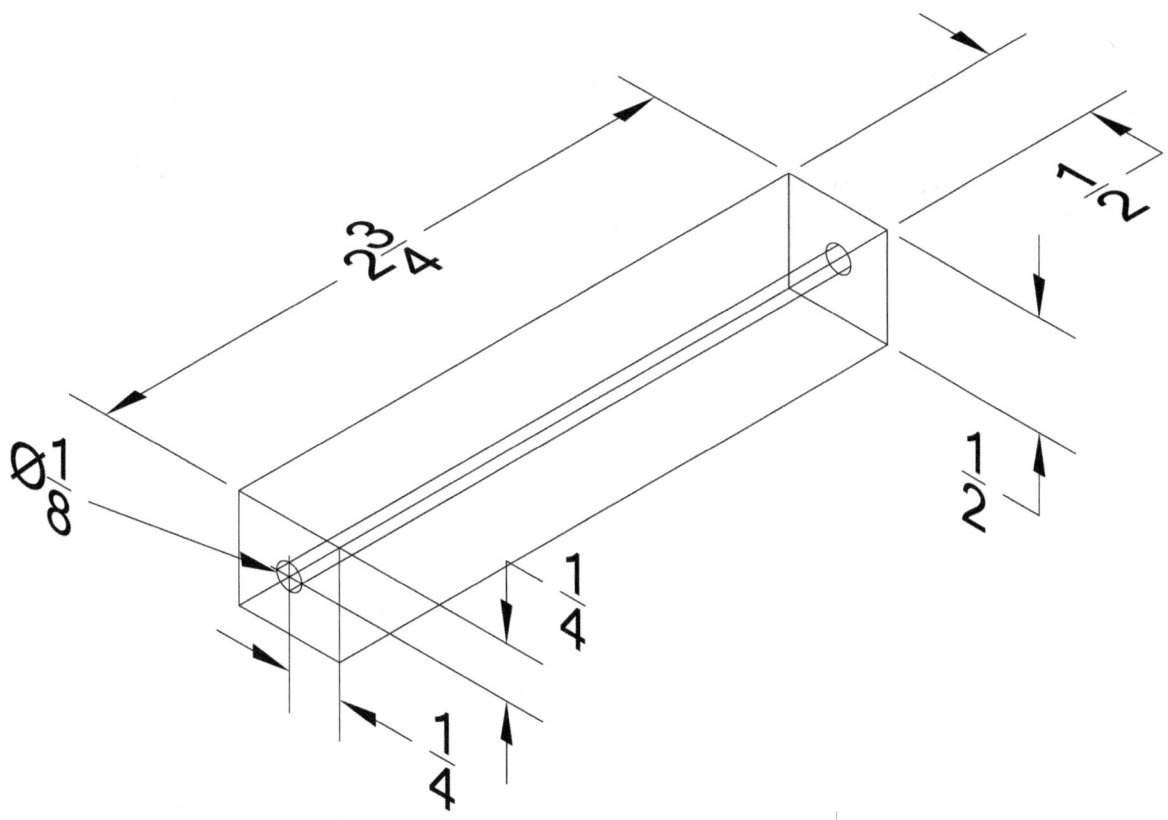

Figure 3.3

The tools used to cut the plate spacers will depend on what you have available. Only the 2-3/4" length is critical. Any saw can be used: a jig saw; scroll saw; band saw; even a chop saw. If you are making a 1/2" x 1/2" spacer, start with 1/2" stock and cut a piece 1/2" wide. Once cut, mark the center of each end by placing marks across the diagonals. Place the spacer against two pieces of scrap to hold it perpendicular while you drill the pilots with your drill press.

If you are going to round over the edges, do that now. Cut six spacers.

Tip
It is important that all the spacers be exactly the same length. The best way to do this is to cut the length of your stock first. Then cut the spacers from that piece.

Thick Spacers

Thick spacers are used on the gear train to help hold some of the gears in place between the clock plates. The thick gears are always used in conjunction with thin spacers when assembling your clock.

The thick spacers shown in Figure 3.4 must be cut from the same stock as your gears. This is important as they must be the same thickness. If you use the templates available on the Kronos Robotics web site, the three thick spacers needed are part of the small gears template.

All thick spacers have the overall dimensions shown in Figure 3.5, provided you are using 1/2" stock for your gears. If you are using some sort of plywood then the thickness will most likely be 11/32"

Figure 3.4

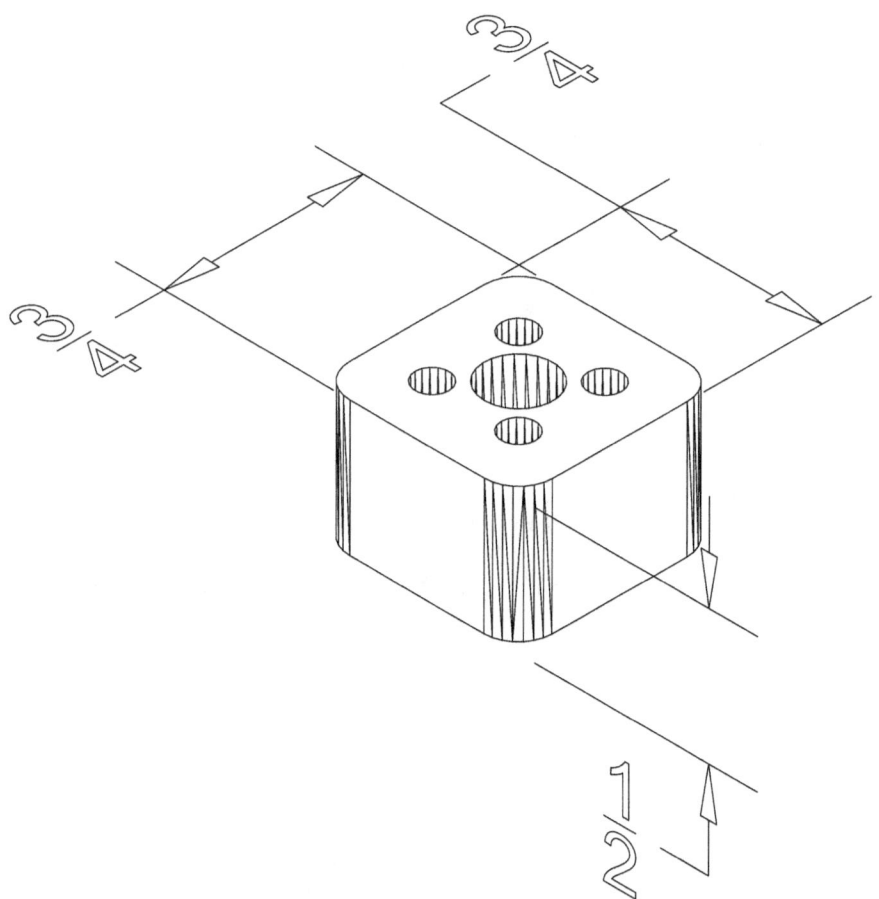

Figure 3.5

Cut two thick spacers with 7/32" center holes and one thick spacer with a 1/4" center hole. If you are using the templates, you will need to enlarge the 1/8" pilot holes to these sizes. On the HANS electric gear clock, the four outer holes are optional, and can be omitted. Use a drill press when drilling the center holes.

You can fillet the edges, as shown in Figure 3.6, using any means you see fit. The safest way is to use a disk sander. The fillets are totally optional and won't effect the operation of your clock.

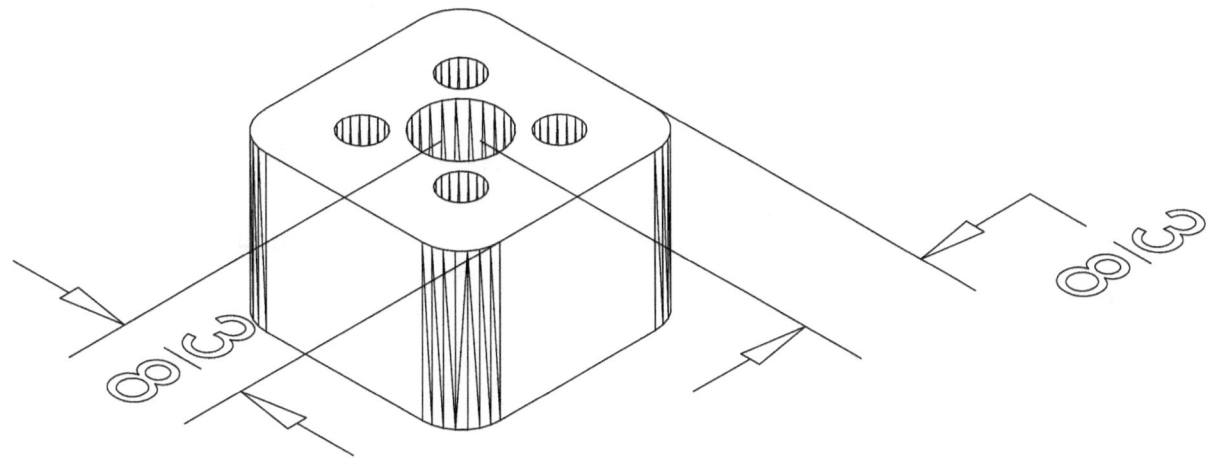

Figure 3.6

Gear Spacers

The three gear spacers shown in Figure 3.7 are used to attach two gears to each other. They are 1/8" and have the same diameters as the two gears they are joining.

The best way to make the spacers is to lay out the outside circle on your stock and mark your center hole. First drill the hole, then go back and cut the circle out with a scroll or band saw. While the four outer holes can be used to align the gears, they are optional.

If you don't want to make the gear spacers, the Kronos Robotics web site sells a set of laser cut spacers.

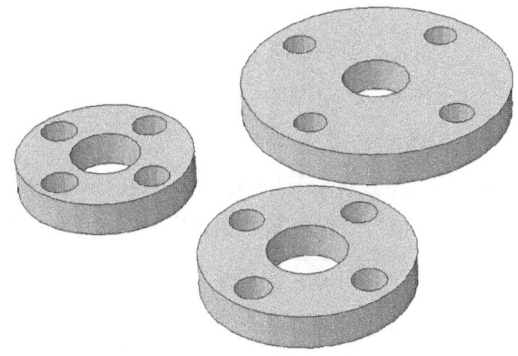

Figure 3.7

Gear Spacer 1

Gear spacer 1 shown in Figure 3.8 is used to attach gear 3 to gear 4. The gear is 5/8" in diameter with a 1/4" center hole.

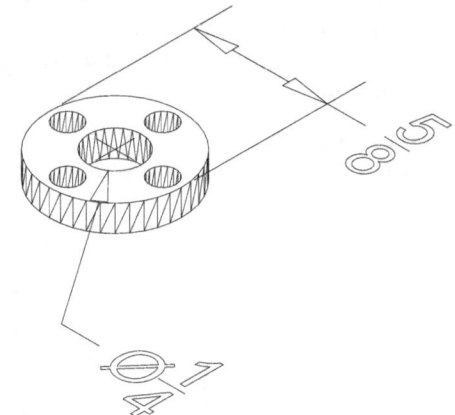

Figure 3.8

Gear Spacer 2

Gear spacer 2 shown in Figure 3.9 is used to attach gear 5 to gear 6. The gear is 1" in diameter with a 1/4" center hole.

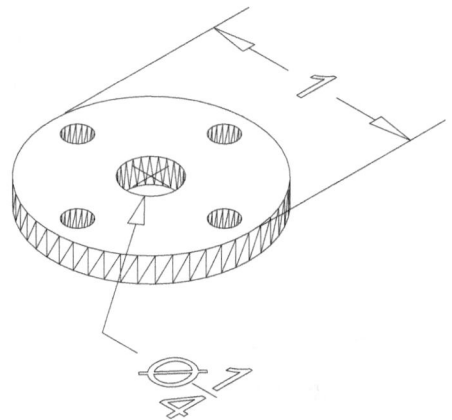

Figure 3.9

Gear Spacer 3

Gear spacer 3 shown in Figure 3.10 is used to attach gear 7 to gear 8. The gear is 3/4" in diameter with a 9/32" center hole.

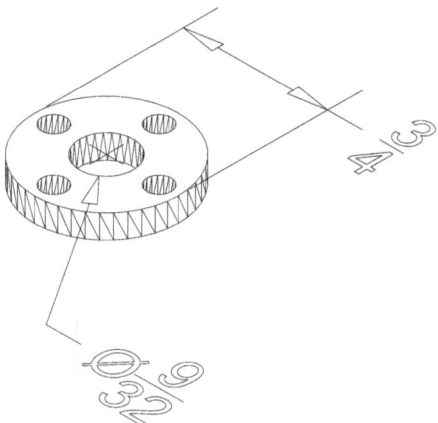

Figure 3.10

Thin Spacers

Thin spacers are used in conjunction with the thick spacers and as simple bushings to allow gears to turn freely.

One of the thin spacers has an undersized hole and small slit, and is used to hold a gear in place. As with the gear spacers, they are 1/8" thick and should be constructed in the same manner.

All thin spacers are 1/2" in diameter. The following thin spacers will be needed to complete the clock:

- 10, 1/2" diameter spacers with a 7/32" center hole
- 5, 1/2" diameter spacers with a 1/4" center hole
- 1, 1/2" diameter spacer with a 9/32" center hole
- 1, 1/2" diameter spacer with a .24" center hole

The last spacer is a locking spacer used to hold gear 7 in place. You can use a 15/64" drill bit to drill the center hole. The slit is optional and can be omitted when using a 15/64 drill bit.

Note that all the thin spacer dimensions are not critical, with the exception of the locking spacer, which must be tight.

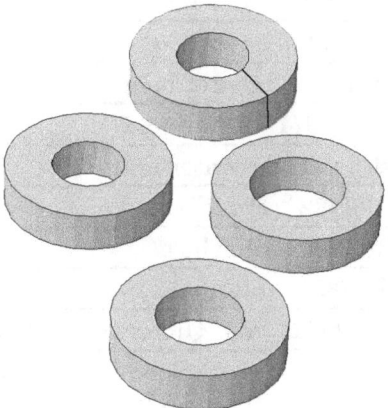

Figure 3.11

Conclusion

As you build the spacers, label them so you can select the proper spacer when assembling the clock. Refer to Appendix A to help with the labeling. All the spacers can be marked on the face, as it will not show when assembled.

The drawings of the spacer, are provided single sided so that they can be copied. This will allow you to tape or glue them to your stock for cutting and drilling.

In order to help you keep track of all the spacers needed to build HANS, the following table has been provided.

Use Table 3.1 to keep track of all the spacers used in building the HANS electric gear clock.

Qty	**Spacer**
6	1/2" x 1/2" x 2-3/4" Plate Spacers
2	Thick spacers with 1/4" center holes
1	Thick spacer with 9/32" center hole
1	Gear spacer 1 with a 1/4" center hole
1	Gear spacer 2 with a 1/4" center hole
1	Gear spacer 3 with a 9/32" center hole
10	Thin spacers with 7/32" center hole
5	Thin spacers with 1/4" center hole
1	Thin spacer with 9/32" center hole
1	Thin spacer with .24" (15/64" OK) center hole (lock spacer)

Table 3.1

Chapter 4

Gear Assembly

O nce the gears and spacers are cut, the gears can be assembled. This is done by cutting a brass tube and gluing the gears and spacers in place.

Tools Needed For This Chapter

- Metal file
- Razor knife
- Tubing cutter
- Thick CA glue (gap filling)
- Yellow wood glue
- 120 Grit sand paper

Components Needed For This Chapter

- All gears #3 - #9
- Gear spacers #1 - #3
- 1/4" Brass tubing
- 9/32" Brass tubing

Prerequisites

All gears and spacers should be cut and the center holes sized as indicated in the last two chapters. Each piece of tubing will be cut as needed while assembling the gears, so have the brass tubing readily available.

Step 1 - Assemble Gears 3 and 4

The following parts are needed to assemble gears 3 and 4:

- Gear 3, 60 tooth gear
- Gear 4, 8 tooth gear
- Gear spacer 1
- 1/4" Brass tube 1-1/8" long

Assembly involves gluing the tube into the large 60 tooth gear, then gluing the spacer in place, and finally gluing the 8 tooth gear in place, as shown in Figure 4.1.

Figure 4.1

Step 1A

Cut a piece of 1/4" brass rod to a 1-1/8" length, as shown in Figure 4.2. It's ok if the tube is a little shorter, but not longer.

Before proceeding, clean all the burs from the inside and outside edges of the cut tubing.

Once cut and cleaned, rough up the surface of the tubing with 120 grit sand paper. This will allow the thick CA glue to hold better.

Place a couple of drops of CA glue on the tube near the edge to be inserted.

Insert the tube into the gear. With the gear flat on a table surface, use a piece of wood scrap to press the gear until it is flush with the bottom of the gear.

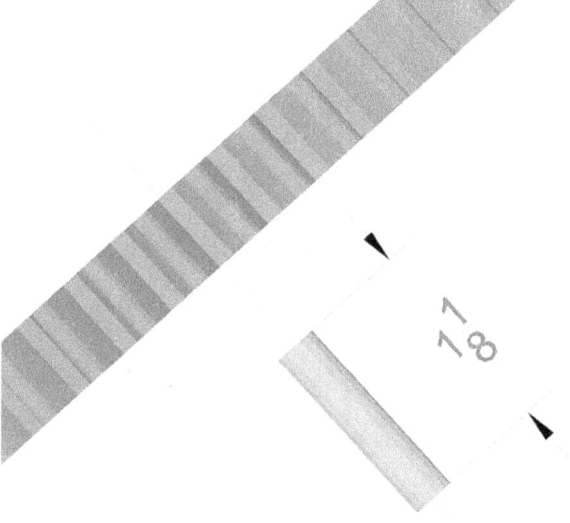

Figure 4.2

Step 1B

Place a thin coat of yellow wood glue on both sides of gear spacer #1, and slip it on the brass tube, as shown in Figure 4.3.

If your gears and spacers have holes, you can roughly align them. This will allow the glue to act as a lock when the glue has dried.

Figure 4.3

Step 1C

Place a couple of drops of CA glue on the exposed portion of the brass tube.

Slip the 8 tooth gear over the tube, roughly aligning the holes if present, and press in place using a piece of scrap wood. The gear should be seated against the 1/4" gear spacer, as shown in Figure 4.4.

Use a knife or cotton swab to remove any glue that may have gotten on the inside of the tube.

Figure 4.4

Step 2 - Assemble Gears 7 and 8

The following parts are needed to assemble gears 7 and 8:

- Gear 7, 40 tooth gear
- Gear 8, 10 tooth gear
- Gear spacer #3
- 9/32" Brass tube 15/16" long

Assembly involves gluing the tube into the smaller 10 tooth gear, then gluing the spacer in place, and finally gluing the 40 tooth gear in place, as shown in Figure 4.5.

The assembly process for this set of gears has been reversed due to the pocket in the center of the gear 7.

Figure 4.5

Step 2A

Cut a piece of 9/32" brass tubing to a length of 15/16", as shown in Figure 4.6. Clean up all the burs from both the inside and outside edges of the tubing.

Using 120 grit sand paper, rough the entire outside of the tube.

Place a couple of drops of CA glue on the tube near the edge to be inserted.

Insert the tube into the gear. With the gear flat on a table surface, use a piece of wood scrap to press the gear until is flush with the bottom of the gear.

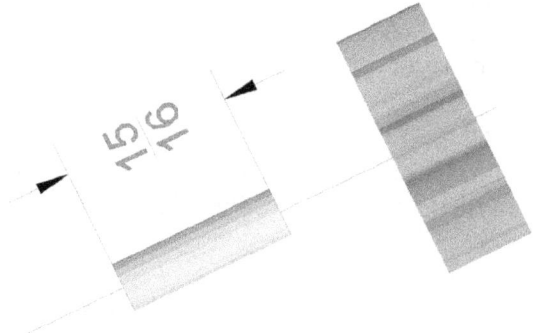

Figure 4.6

Step 2B

Place a thin coat of yellow wood glue on both sides of gear spacer #3, and slip it on the brass tube, as shown in Figure 4.7.

If your gears and spacers have holes, you can roughly align them. This will allow the glue to act as a lock when the glue has dried.

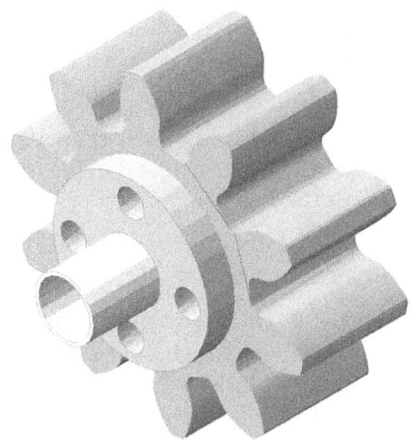

Figure 4.7

Step 2C

Place a couple drops of CA glue on the exposed portion of the brass tube.

Slip the 40 tooth gear over the tube and press in place using a piece of scrap wood. The gear should be seated against the gear spacer, as shown in Figure 4.8.

Use a knife or cotton swab to remove any glue that may have gotten on the inside of the tube.

Figure 4.8

Building the Hans Electric Gear Clock

Step 3 - Assemble Gear 9

Cut a piece of 9/32" brass tubing to a length of 1-7/8". Clean up all the burs from the tubing.

Using 120 grit sand paper, rough up the tube, about 1/2" on one end. This will be the end glued to the gear.

Place a couple of drops of CA glue on the tube near the sanded edge.

Insert the tube into the gear, as shown in Figure 4.9. With the gear flat on a table surface, use a piece of wood scrap to press the gear until is flush with the bottom of the gear.

The finished gear should look like the gear shown in Figure 4.10. Be sure to remove any glue that may have gotten on the inside of the tube.

Figure 4.9

Figure 4.10

Step 4 - Assemble Gears 5 and 6

The following parts are needed to assemble gears 5 and 6:

- Gear 5, 64 tooth gear
- Gear 6, 16 tooth gear
- Gear spacer #2
- 1/4" Brass tube 4-7/8" long

Assembly involves gluing the tube into the large 64 tooth gear, then gluing the spacer in place, and finally gluing the 16 tooth gear in place, as shown in Figure 4.11.

Figure 4.11

Step 4A

Cut a piece of 1/4" brass tubing to a length of 4-7/8", as shown in Figure 4.12. Clean up all the burs from the inside and outside edges of the tubing.

Using 120 grit sand paper, rough the center of the tube.

Figure 4.12

Step 4B

Place a mark on the tube 2-15/16" from one end. Consider this the long end of the tube. The portion to be inserted into the gear will be the short end.

Clamp a piece of scrap with a hole to a bench or table. Place the center of gear 5 over the hole and place the short end of the tube in the hole, as shown in Figure 4.13.

With a wooden mallet or hammer and a piece of scrap, drive the tube into the gear until the mark is about 1/2" from the gear, as shown in Figure 4.14.

Place a couple of drops of CA glue on the tube at about 1/2" below the line. Drive the tube into the gear until the line touches the gear as shown in Figure 4.15.

Figure 4.13

Figure 4.14

It is important that any excess CA glue is wiped from the gear. Let the CA glue dry for about 15 minutes before proceeding to the next step.

Figure 4.15

Step 4C

Place a thin coat of yellow wood glue on both sides of gear spacer #2 and slip it on the brass tube, as shown in Figure 4.16.

Figure 4.16

Step 4D

Place gear 6 with its center over the hole and insert the long end of the tube/gear assembly into the center hole, as shown in Figure 4.17.

Using a wooden mallet or hammer and scrap, drive the tubing into gear 6 until it is about 1/2" from the gear spacer that you just installed.

Place a couple of drops of CA glue on the tube just above gear 6 and drive it the rest of the way. You should be able to feel when the gears come in contact with each other.

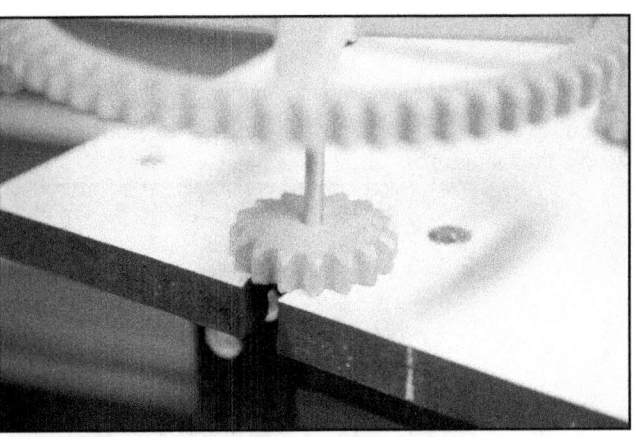

Figure 4.17

Building the Hans Electric Gear Clock **43**

The finished assembly should look like the one shown in Figure 4.18. There should be about 2-5/16" of the tube sticking out past gear 6. If you are within 1/8", you should be ok.

Figure 4.18

Conclusion

This completes the gear assemblies. The finished assemblies shown in Figure 4.19, will be used later when you assemble the clock.

Figure 4.19

44   Chapter 4   Gear Assembly

Chapter 5

Clock Face and Hands

The clock face and hands are what give a clock most of its personality. The clock maker has a great deal of freedom when designing the clock face and hands. This is also true with HANS.

Tools Needed For This Chapter

- Scroll saw (see text)
- Yellow wood glue
- 120 Grit sandpaper

Components Needed For This Chapter

- 1, 12" x 24" piece of 1/8" hardboard

Prerequisites

Refer to the drawings in Appendix A. Scaled drawings of the face and hands are provided. You may have to make multiple copies of the face in order to piece together a full size drawing. It all depends on the capacity of the copier you are using.

The clock face originally was made from three pieces of 1/8" hardboard or MDF. It consists of the main face and two rings that are glued on. These rings are not necessary and can be omitted if you wish. The thickness of the main face can also be made from 1/4" stock. If you are using any material other than MDF or hardboard you may want to use a 1/4" thickness for stability.

There are three ways of creating the face:

1. Cut the main face with a band saw or scroll saw and glue digits to it
2. Cut the main face and digits with a scroll saw
3. Purchase a laser cut set from the Kronos Robotics web site

You may redesign the clock face to any size or shape. The critical points are the four mounting holes because they must line up with the clock plate. A drawing of the clock face has been provided in Appendix A. Since the face is nearly 12" x 12", grid lines have been provided so that multiple copies may be made and attached in order to create the proper sized drawing. Note that this only needs to be done if you are using the drawing as a template.

The following instructions assume that you have cut the face and rings or purchased a set from the Kronos Robotics web site.

Step 1 - Position Main Face

Lay the main face on a flat surface, as shown in Figure 5.1. You want the front of the face pointing up.

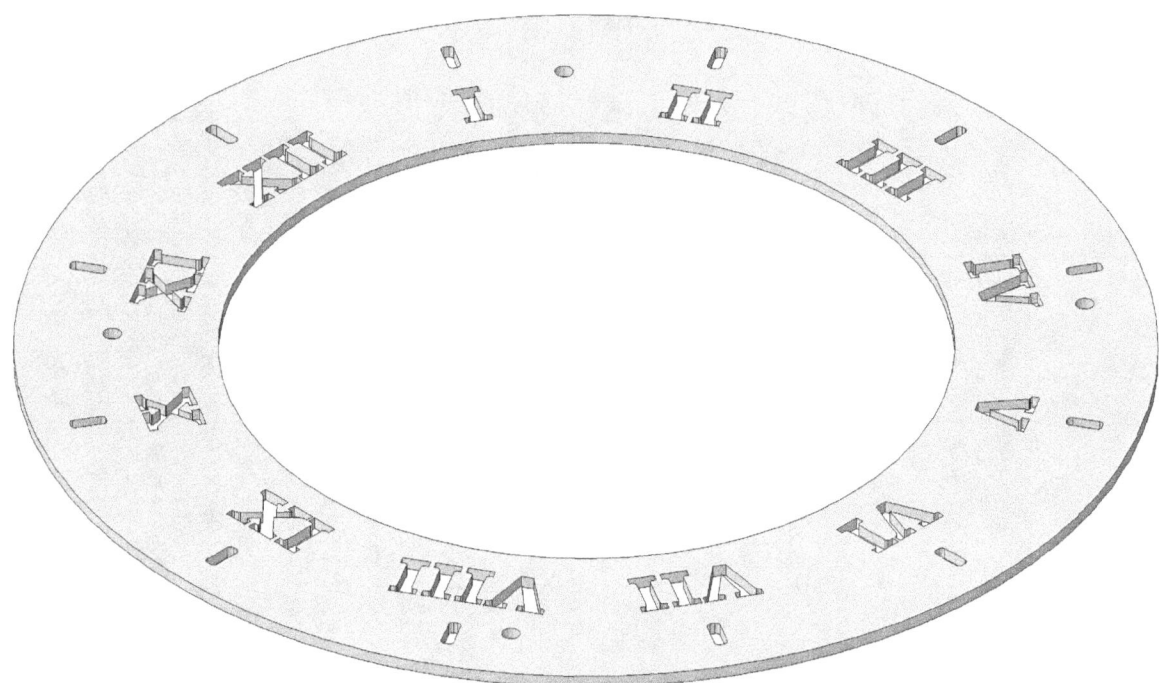

Figure 5.1

Step 2 - Attach Inner Ring

Place a thin layer of yellow wood glue on the smaller ring and carefully attach it to the main face, as shown in Figure 5.2. The inside edges of the ring and the main face should be flush.

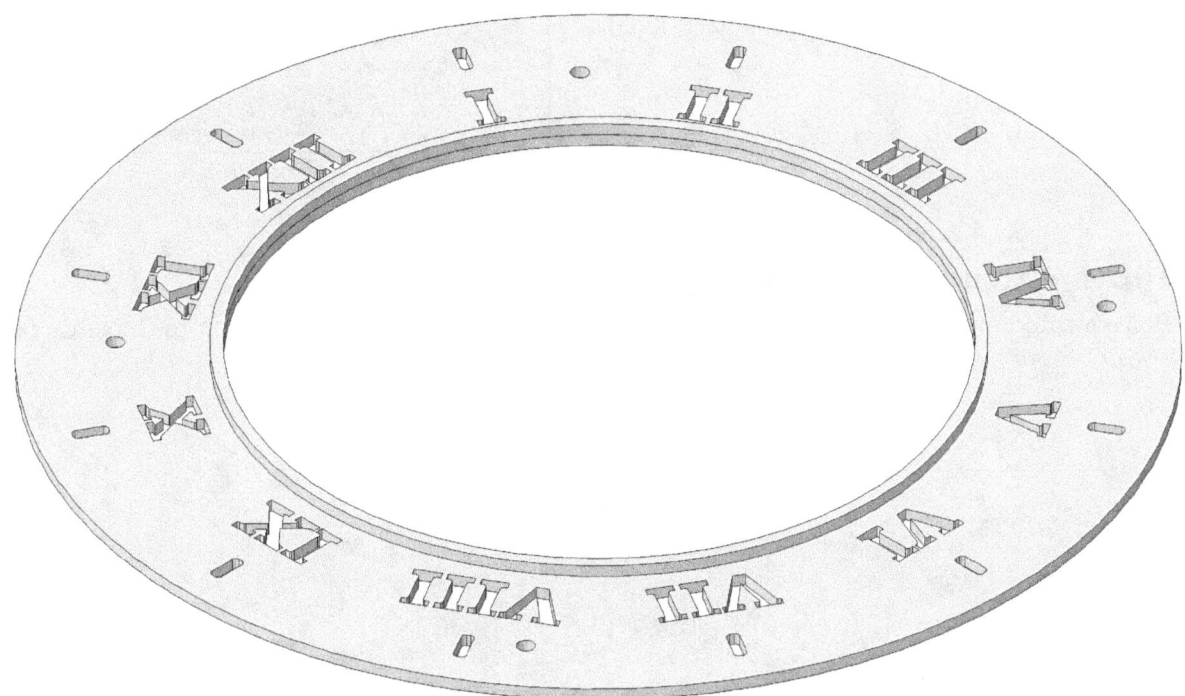

Figure 5.2

Tip

Use the corner of a piece of scrap to align the inside edges of the inner ring with the main clock face, as shown in Figure 5.3.

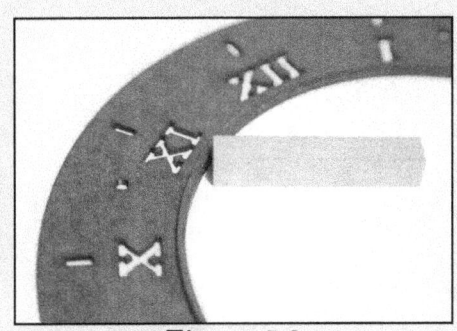

Figure 5.3

Building the Hans Electric Gear Clock

Step 3 - Add Weight to the Face

To clamp the ring to the face, add some weight to the inner ring, as shown in Figure 5.4.

Apply the weight carefully, as not to affect the position of the inner ring.

Let the glue set for 30 minutes, then remove the weight and clean up the excess glue with a chisel or scraper.

Figure 5.4

Step 4 - Attach Outer Ring

Place a thin layer of yellow wood glue on the larger ring and carefully attach it to the main face, as shown in Figure 5.5. The outside edges of the ring and the main face should be flush.

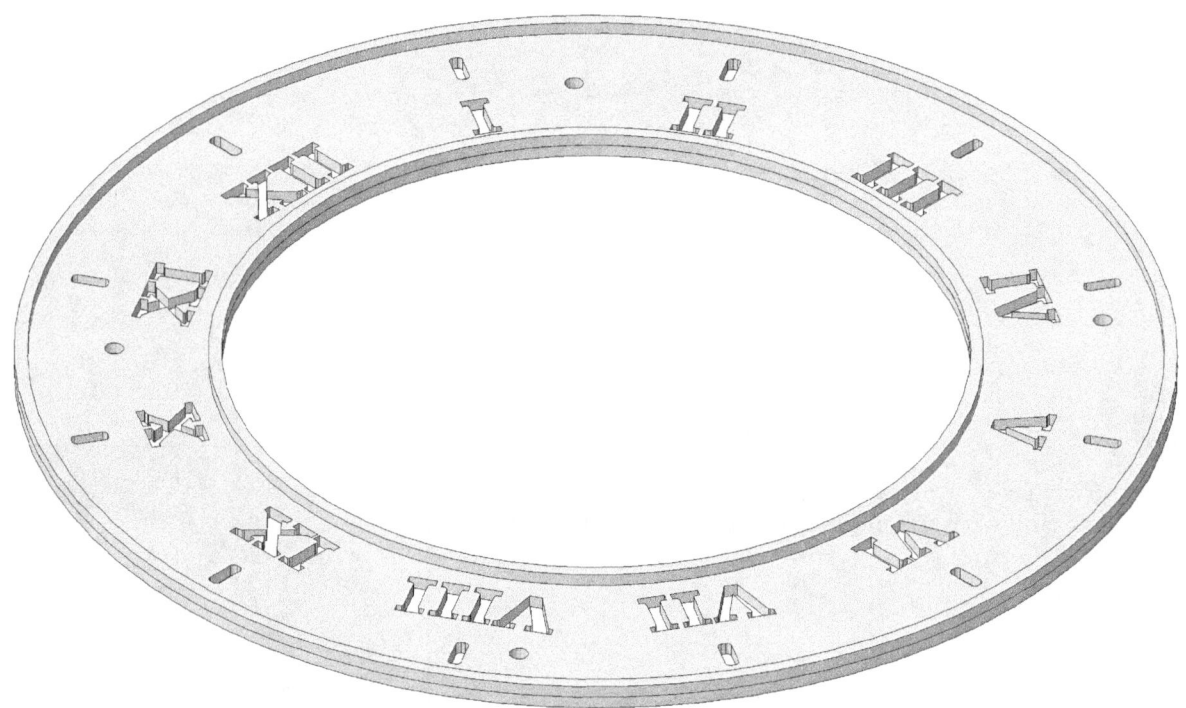

Figure 5.5

Use some blue painter's tape to hold the ring in place, as shown in Figure 5.6.

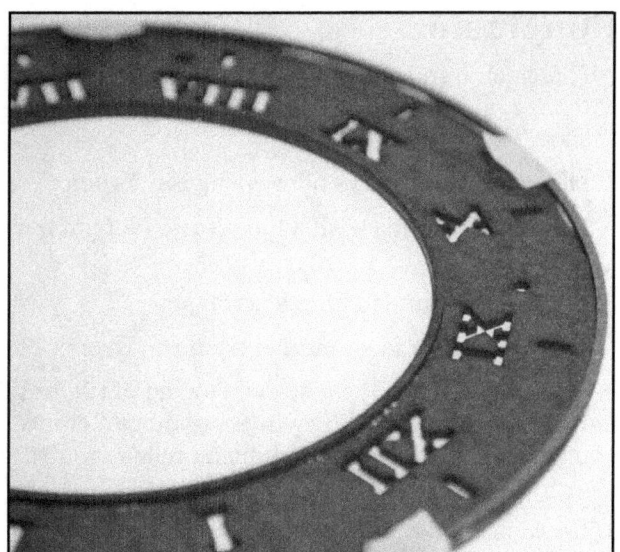

Figure 5.6

Step 5 - Add Weight to the Face

Add enough weight to cover the outer ring.

Let the glue set for 30 minutes, then remove the weight and clean up the excess glue with a chisel or scraper.

Step 6 - Clean the Face

Let the finished face dry for a few hours, then take some 120 grit sandpaper and sand the inner and outer edges. Set the face aside as it will not be used until final assembly.

Conclusion

The clock hands should be made from 1/8" stock. They can be made from any material; however, if you are making them using hardwood, be sure the grain runs the length of the hand and increase the thickness to 1/4".

There are three ways of creating the hands:

1. Cut the hands with a band saw. Note: if using a band saw you will not be able to make the inside cuts
2. Cut the hands using a scroll saw
3. Purchase a laser cut set from the Kronos Robotics web site

Appendix A contains a scaled rawing of the hands (also shown in Figure 5.7). You can create a set of hands based on those drawings or you can create your own. You may also scale the hands to any size you wish. Make sure the mounting holes are drilled to the sizes shown.

Once the hands have been cut, set them aside as they wont be used until final assembly. Note that a 1/2" cap is shown. This cap is glued to the minute hand as a finishing touch and is covered in Chapter 8.

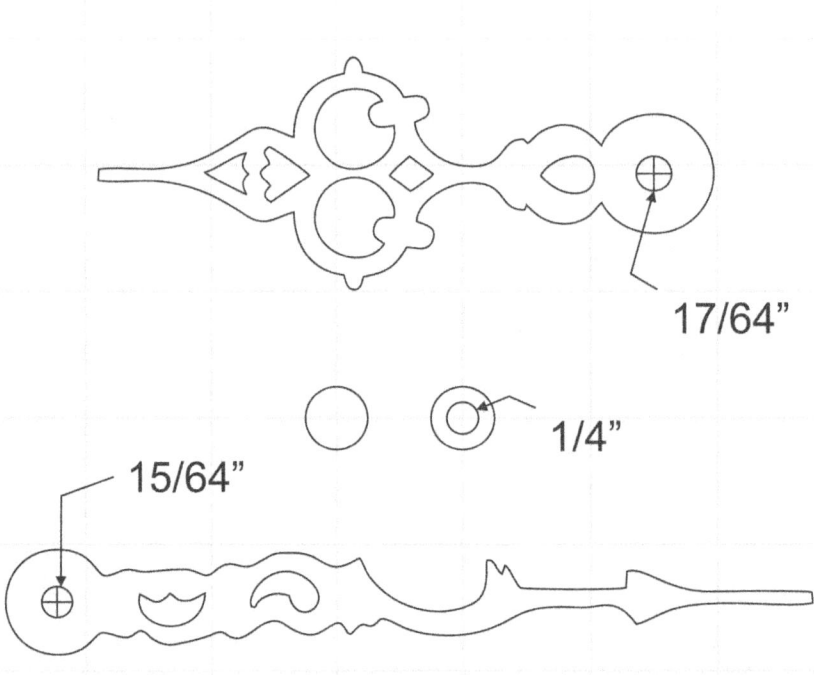

Figure 5.7

Chapter 6

Clock Plates

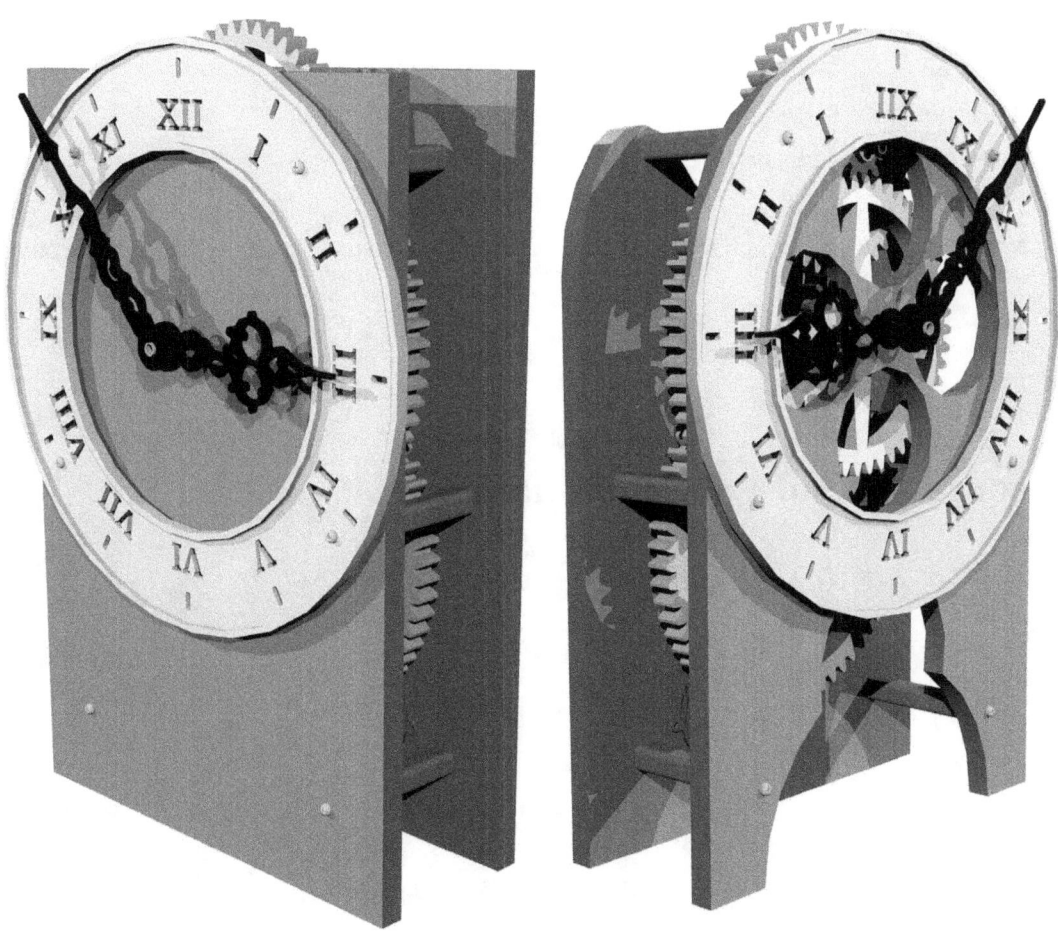

The clock plates are used to enclose the gears. These can be as simple as square planks or rounded and curved shapes to form a unique design. HANS utilizes a unique design that will let you effect the overall appearance of the clock by changing the plate design.

Tools Needed For This Chapter

- Center punch
- Layout tools (see text)
- Drill press
- Dial calipers
- Power drill
- 7/32", 9/32" Drill bits
- 1/8", 3/16", 1/4", 7/16" Drill bits
- 2" Forstner bit
- 1-1/2" Forstner bit
- Scroll saw, jig saw, band saw (see text)

The design type may dictate which saw you use. It is possible to use Forstner bits or hole saws to cut out the plate design.

Components Needed For This Chapter

- 2, pieces of 10" x 15-1/4" stock to form the front and rear plates

Prerequisites

Your gears should be cut and assembled. The spacers should be cut.

You will need to lay out the clock plates. As a minimum, you need a tape measure with 1/32" marks, but a better choice would be a precision marking tool like the one shown in Figure 6.1.

Figure 6.1

Step 1 - Basic Plate Layout

The front and rear plates for HANS are based on a 10" x 15-1/4" cutout of 1/2" stock. You can use the drawings provided in Appendix A or you can lay them out yourself. The advantage of laying the plates out yourself is that you can create variations.

Figure 6.2 shows the basic hole layout for both the front and rear plates. The holes shown are used in conjunction with the plate spacers to tie the two plates together.

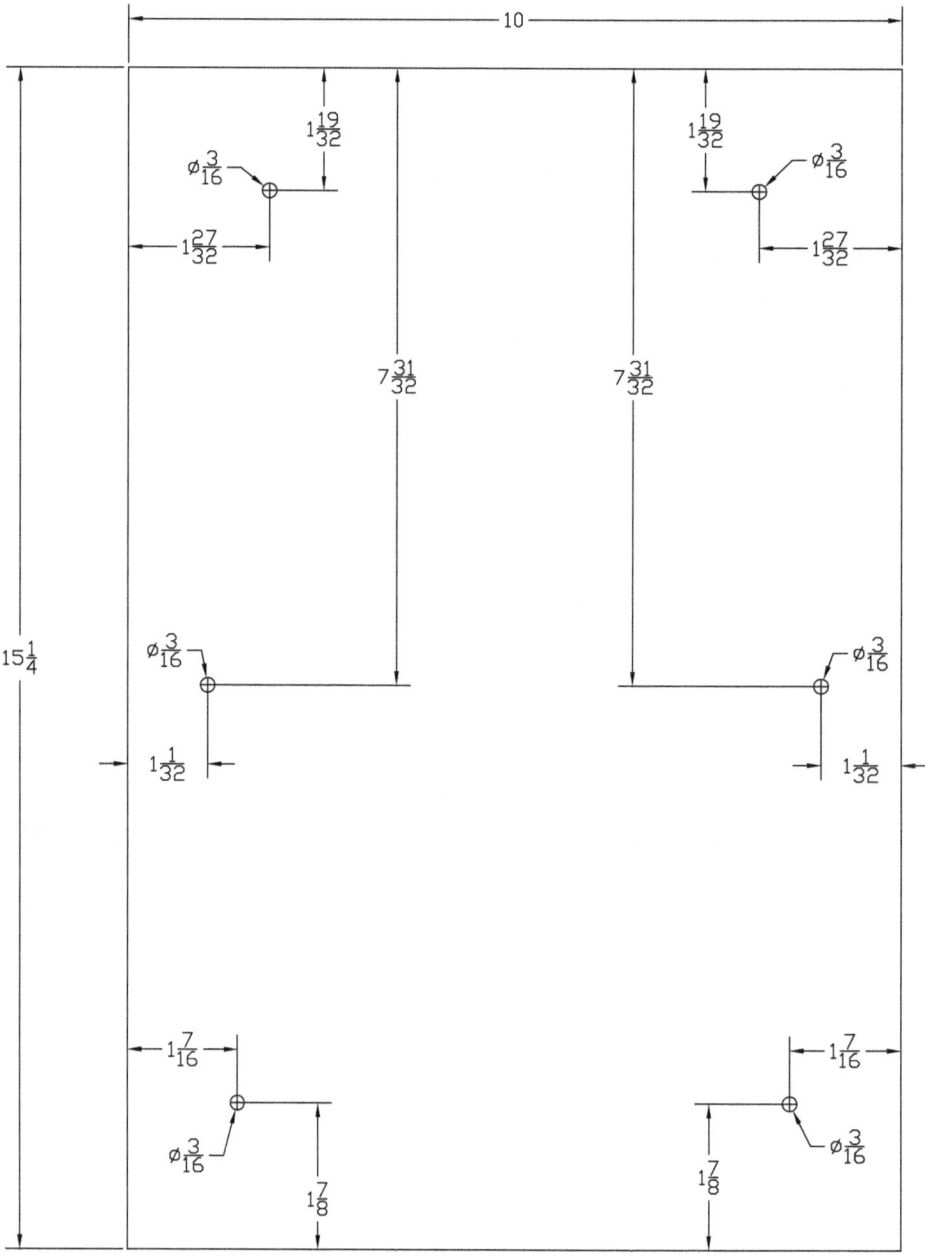

Figure 6.2

56   *Chapter 6*   Clock Plates

Cut two 10" x 15-1/4" pieces out of 1/2" stock, then lay out the holes shown in Figure 6.2.

Step 2 - Drill Plate Spacer Holes

Use a drill press and drill the six, 3/16" holes shown in Figure 6.3. When drilling holes, be sure to place a piece of scrap under your stock. This will keep the bit from blowing out the bottom of your stock.

Figure 6.3

Tip

After laying out your holes, use a center punch to dent the mark, as shown in Figure 6.4. Once dented, the bit will automatically center on the dent. Brad point bits work the best with dented marks,

Figure 6.4

Step 3 - Layout Front Plate Arbor Holes

Lay out the three arbor holes shown in Figure 6.5. Be sure the orientation is correct before marking the holes.

Important: Do not drill the 1/4" and 7/32" holes all the way through. Be sure to read Step 4 thoroughly before drilling any of the arbor holes.

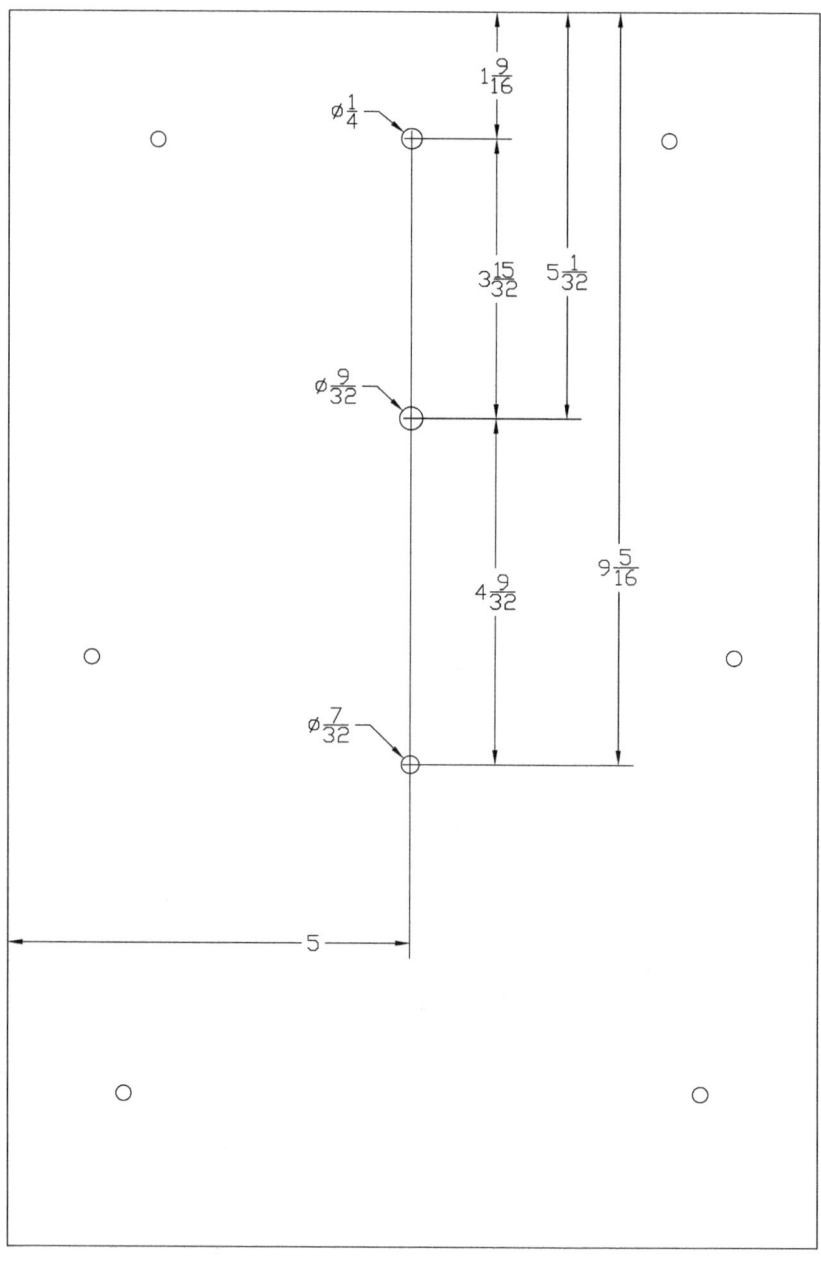

Figure 6.35

Step 4 - Drill Front Plate Arbor Holes

Using a drill press, drill the three center holes shown in Figure 6.6.

The 1/4" hole on the top and the 7/32" hole on the bottom are *not* drilled all the way through the stock. The holes are .4" deep. Use a set of dial calipers to check the depth. It is recommended that you set the depth of your drill press by using a piece of scrap before drilling your plate stock.

The 9/32" hole should be enlarged slightly as the arbor for gear 9 needs to turn freely. You can widen the hole by using a 19/64 drill bit or by using a 9/32" bit and moving the board up and down.

Check the hole by placing a 9/32" thin spacer on the gear 9 assembly and inserting it in the center hole. It should spin freely.

Figure 6.6

Step 5 - Layout Rear Plate Arbor Holes

Lay out the two arbor holes as shown in Figure 6.7. Be sure the orientation is correct before marking the holes.

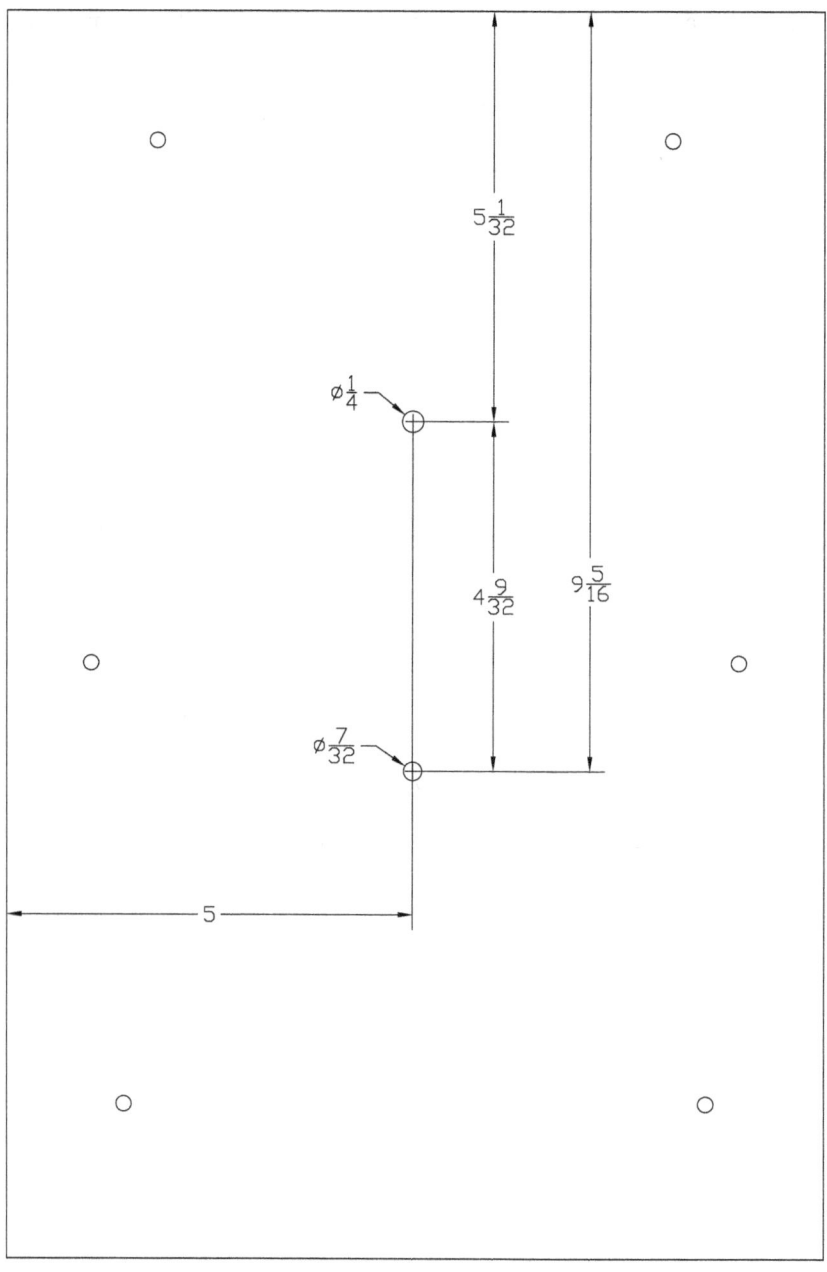

Figure 6.7

60 *Chapter 6*   Clock Plates

Step 6 - Drill Rear Plate Arbor Holes

Using a drill press drill, the two center holes shown in Figure 6.8.

Both holes should be slightly enlarged. For the 1/4" hole you can use a 17/64" drill bit, and for the 7/32", a 15/64" drill bit. You can also use the method described in Step 4 if those bits are not available.

Figure 6.8

Step 7 - Layout Rear Plate Motor Mount 1

Two layouts have been provided to support various syncron motors. Motor mount 1 is the most common, as sources for this motor is provided in the assembly chapters.

Lay out the motor mount holes as shown in Figure 6.9. Be sure the orientation is correct before marking the holes.

The motor mount holes shown here are on the lower left corner of the rear plate. Essentially, you are laying out four holes.

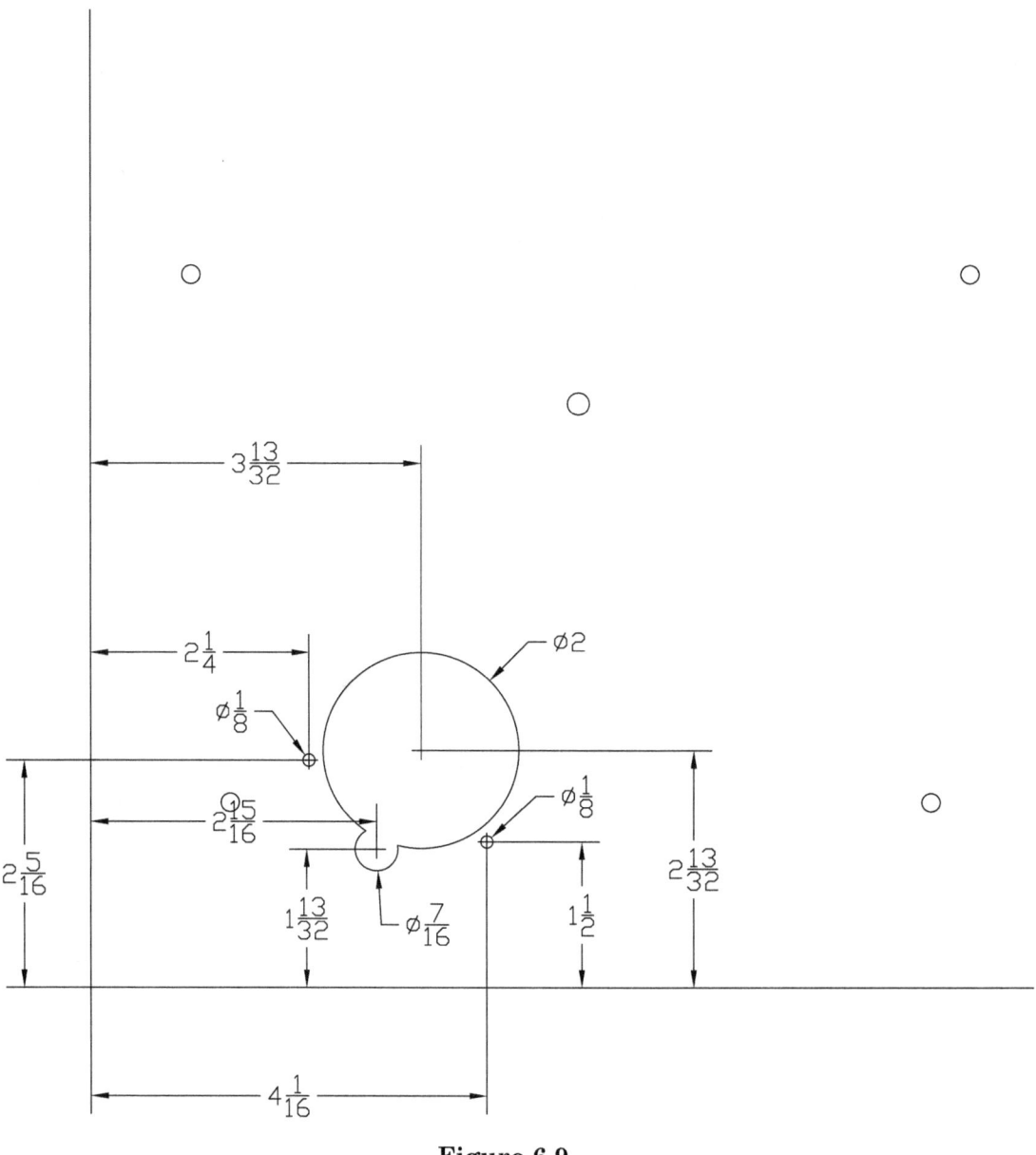

Figure 6.9

62   Chapter 6   Clock Plates

Step 8 - Drill Rear Plate Motor Mount 1 Holes

The motor mount cutouts shown in Figure 6.10 can be cut by drilling four holes. Start by drilling the two 1/8" holes, which will be used to attach the motor. Next, drill the 7/16" hole. The last hole to be drilled is the large 2" hole. You can cut this with a scroll saw, or you can use a 2" Forstner bit. If you use a 2" Forstner bit, make sure you dent the mark so the bit does not wander.

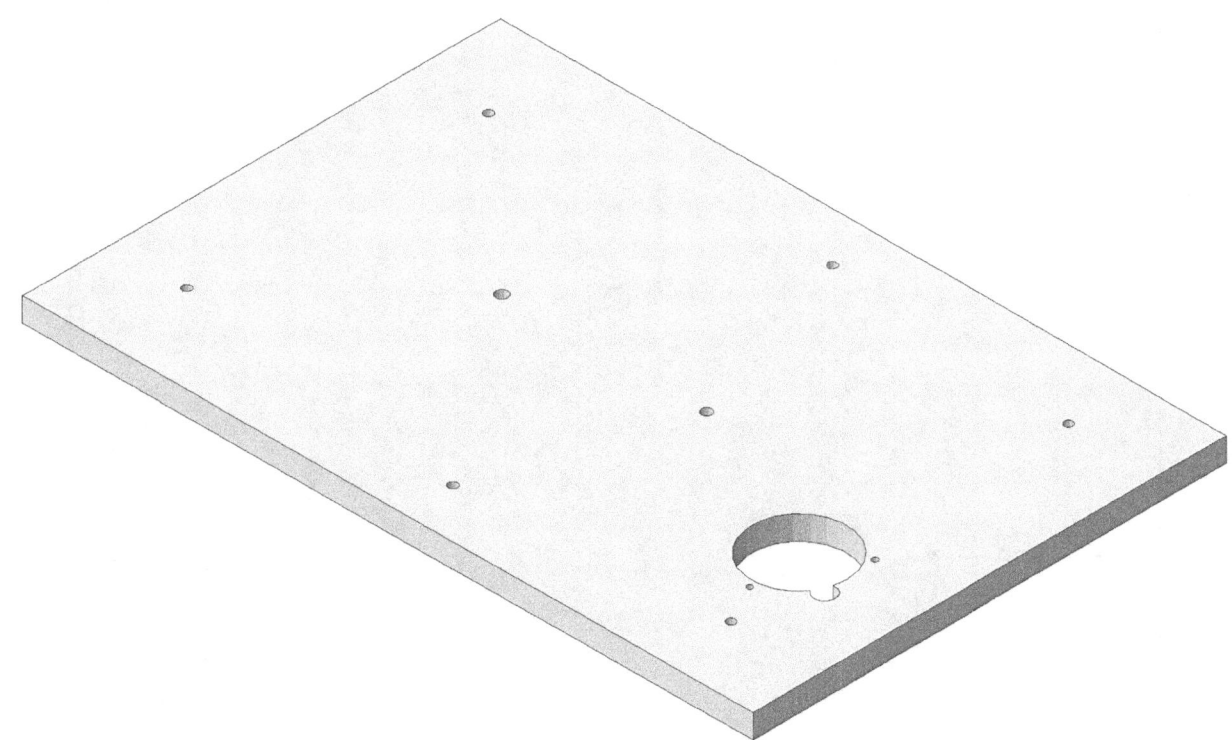

Figure 6.10

Step 9 - Layout Vanity Plate Holes

The vanity plate does two things: it protects the wiring to your motor, and it hides the motor and wiring from view. For safety reasons, always use a vanity plate.

Note that the motor mounting holes have been excluded from the drawing for clarity, as shown in Figure 6.11.

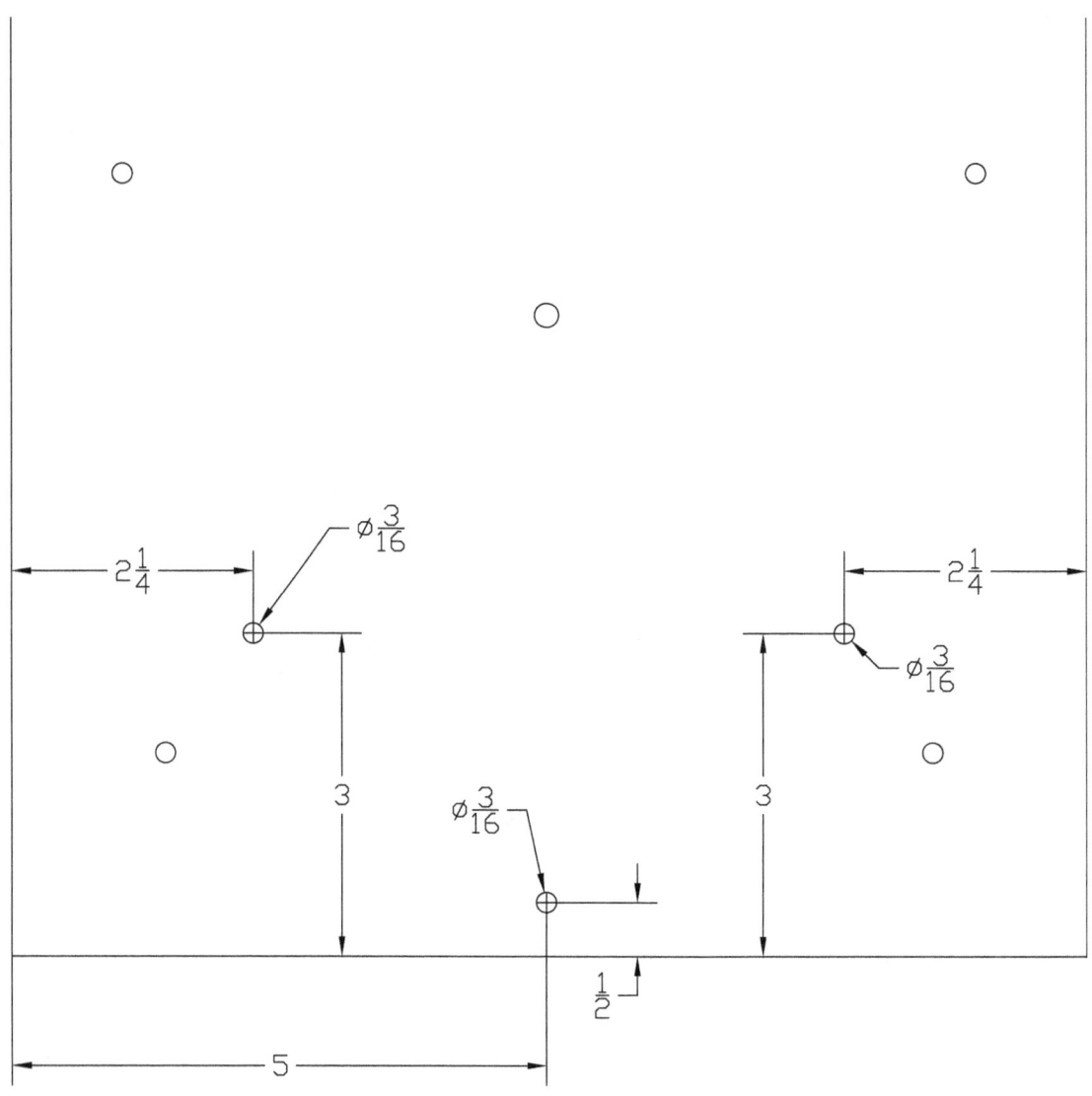

Figure 6.11

64   *Chapter 6*   Clock Plates

Step 10 - Drill Vanity Plate Holes

Using a 3/16" drill bit and a drill press, drill the three vanity plate holes shown in Figure 6.12.

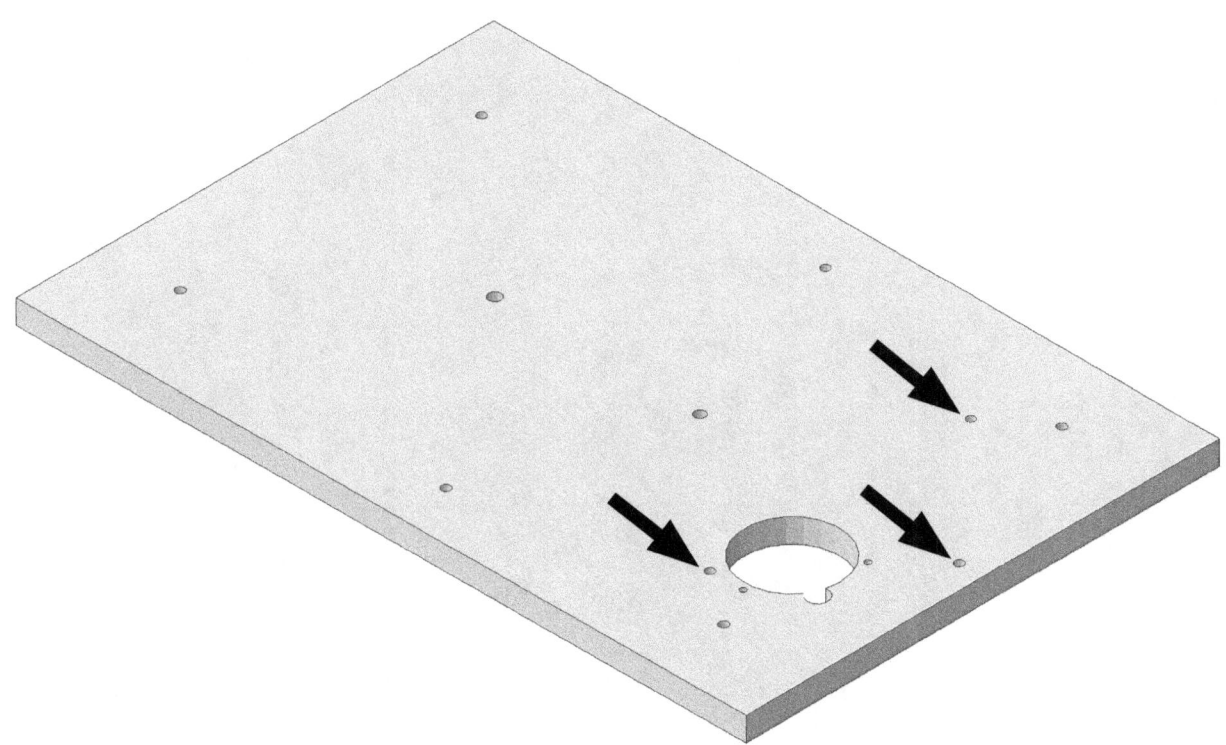

Figure 6.12

Step 9 - Layout Rear Plate Motor Mount 2 (Optional)

Lay out the motor mount holes shown in Figure 6.13. Be sure the orientation is correct before marking the holes.

The motor mount holes shown here are on the lower right corner of the rear plate. Essentially, you are laying out five holes.

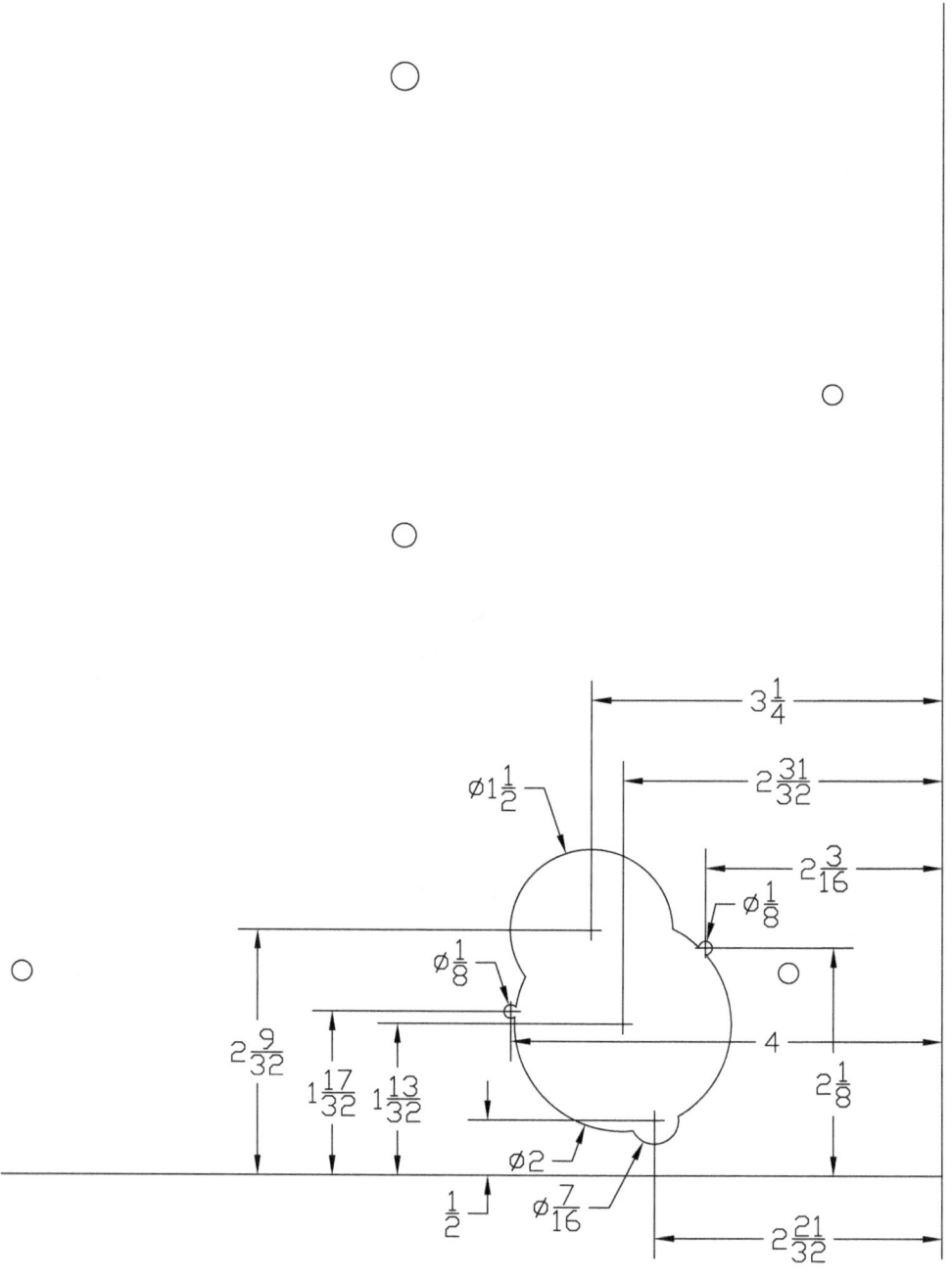

Figure 6.13

Step 10 - Drill Rear Plate Motor Mount 2 Holes

The motor mount cutouts shown in Figure 6.14 can be cut by drilling five holes. Start by drilling the two 1/8" holes. These will be used to attach the motor. Next, drill the 7/16" hole. Use Forstner bits to drill the 1-1/2" and 2" holes, in that order. Dent the holes so the Forstner bit does not wander.

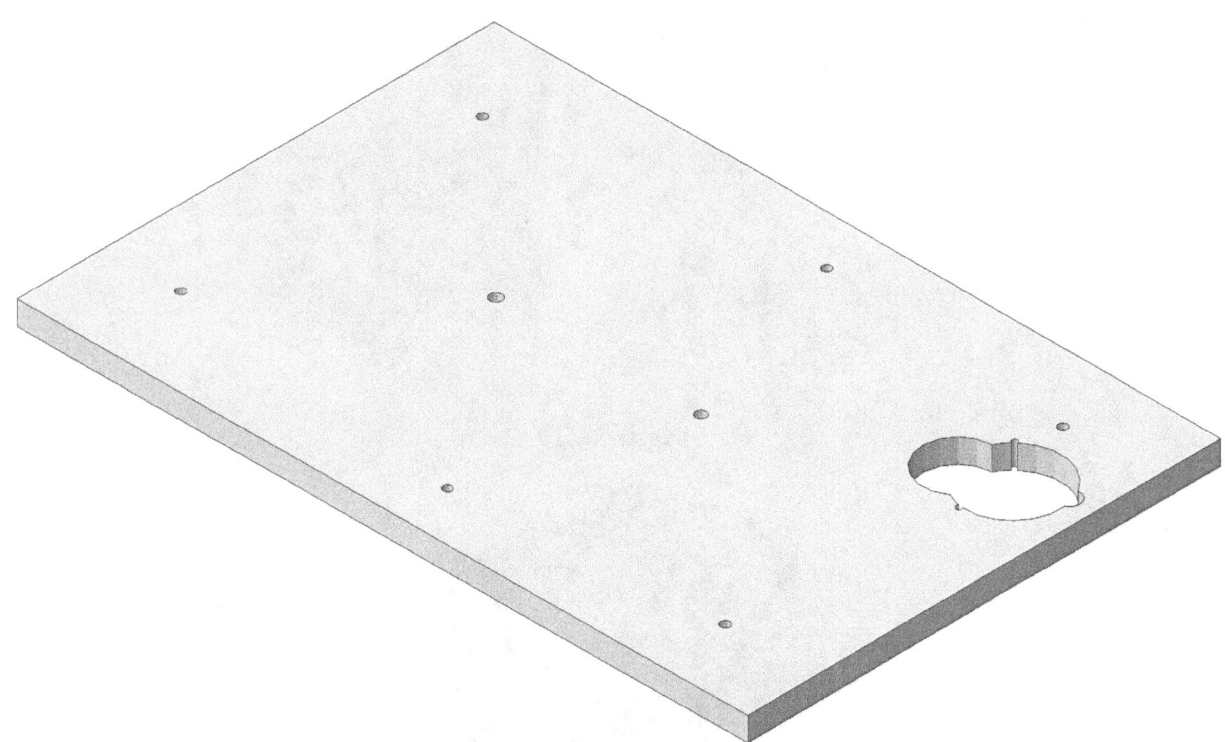

Figure 6.14

The current state of the front and rear plates form the base design for HANS. They are complete enough to actually assemble the clock, as shown in Figure 6.15 and 6.16.

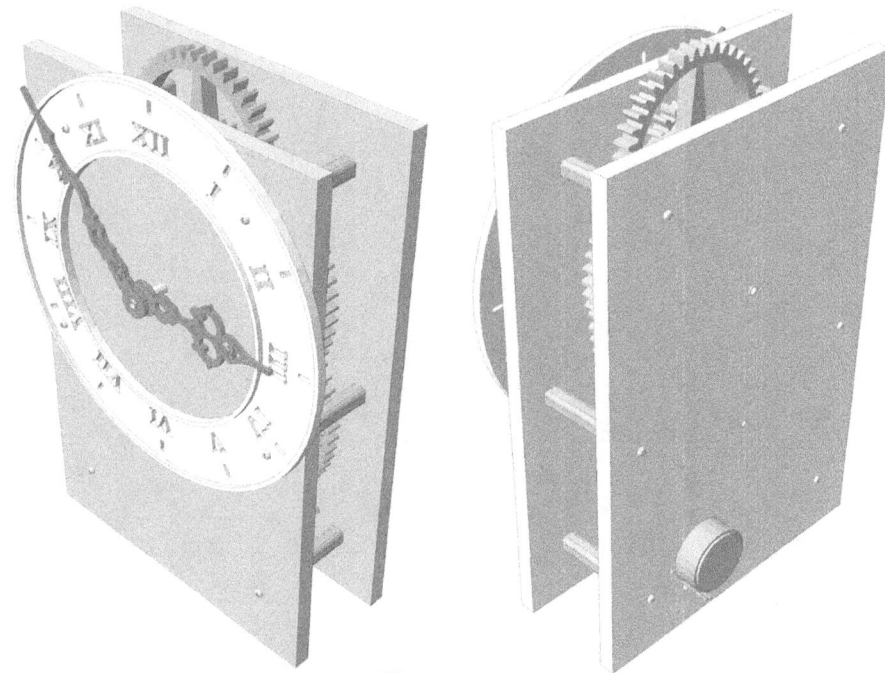

Figure 6.15

Figure 6.16

You can use the drawings in Appendix A to create the traditional HANS clock design, or you can mix things up and play with your own design. You can fillet the corners and cut holes in either the front or rear plate.

There are only two rules:

- The bottoms must form a stand to support the clock
- All the hole small screw hole locations must remain unchanged. Figure 6.17 shows the base plates with some rounded corners and circles cut into the plates. Notice how all the screw holes are still in the proper location. Figure 6.18 shows what the resulting clock would look like.

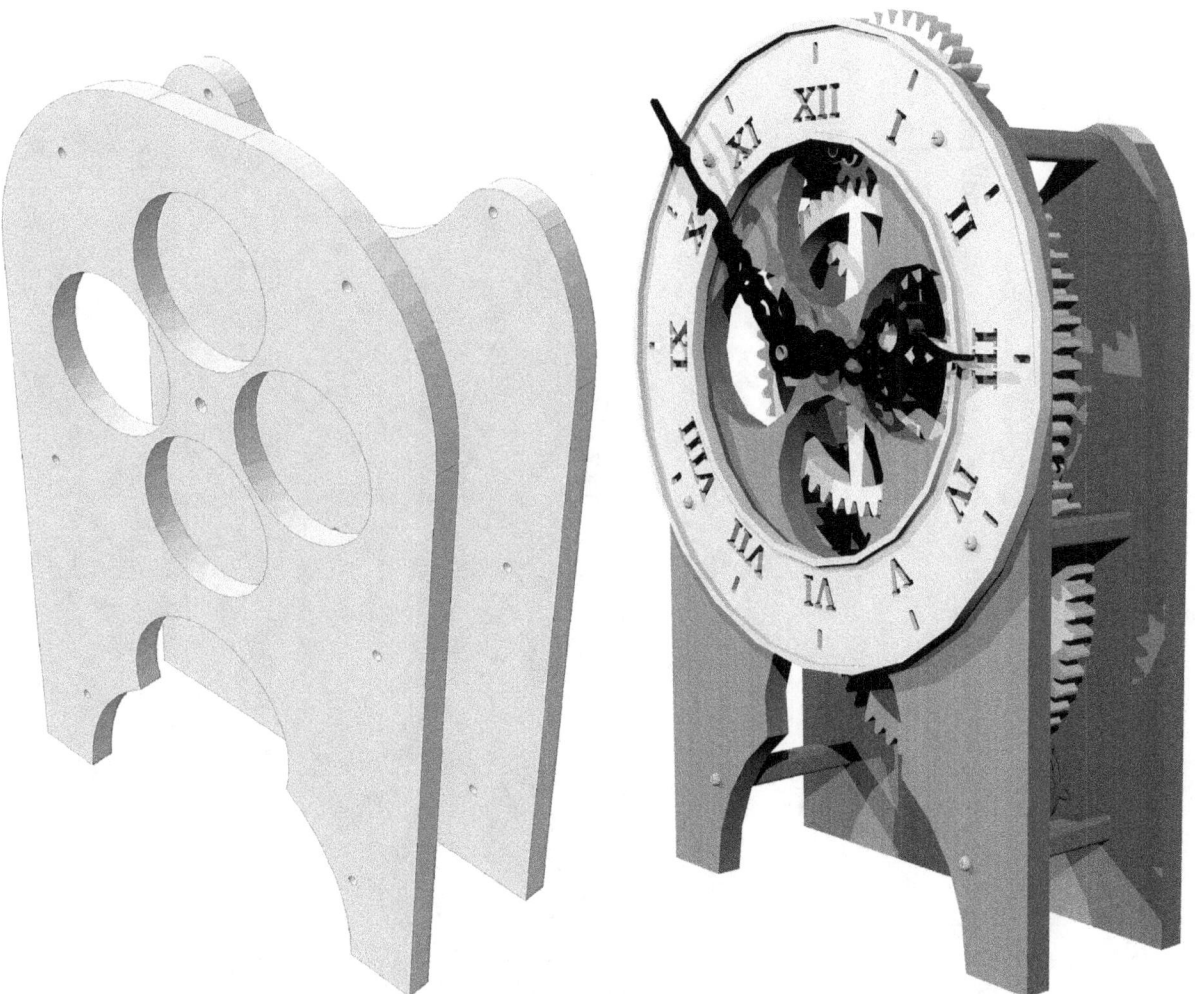

Figure 6.17　　　　　　　　　　Figure 6.18

Step 11 - Layout Vanity Plate

Copy the vanity plate drawings from Appendix A. Tape or glue the drawing to 1/8" stock. Drill the three 3/16" holes first, then cut the plates out with a scroll, band, or jig saw.

Note that you only need one of the plates for your clock. You can use one of these designs or you can create your own. If you do create your own, make sure the hole positions remain unchanged and provide clearance for the plate spacers.

Don't use the drawings shown in Figure 6.19 as they are provided for reference only, and are not scaled properly.

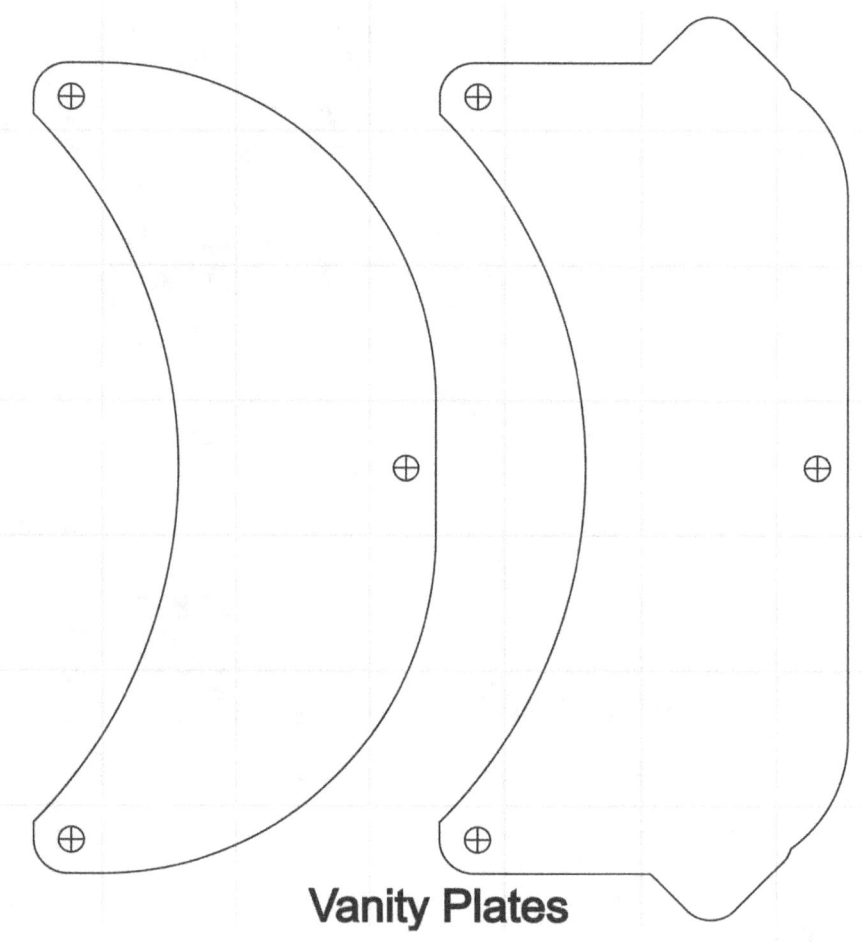

Figure 6.19

The finished vanity plate should look like the plate shown in Figure 6.20. You will be attaching it to the rear plate in the next Chapter.

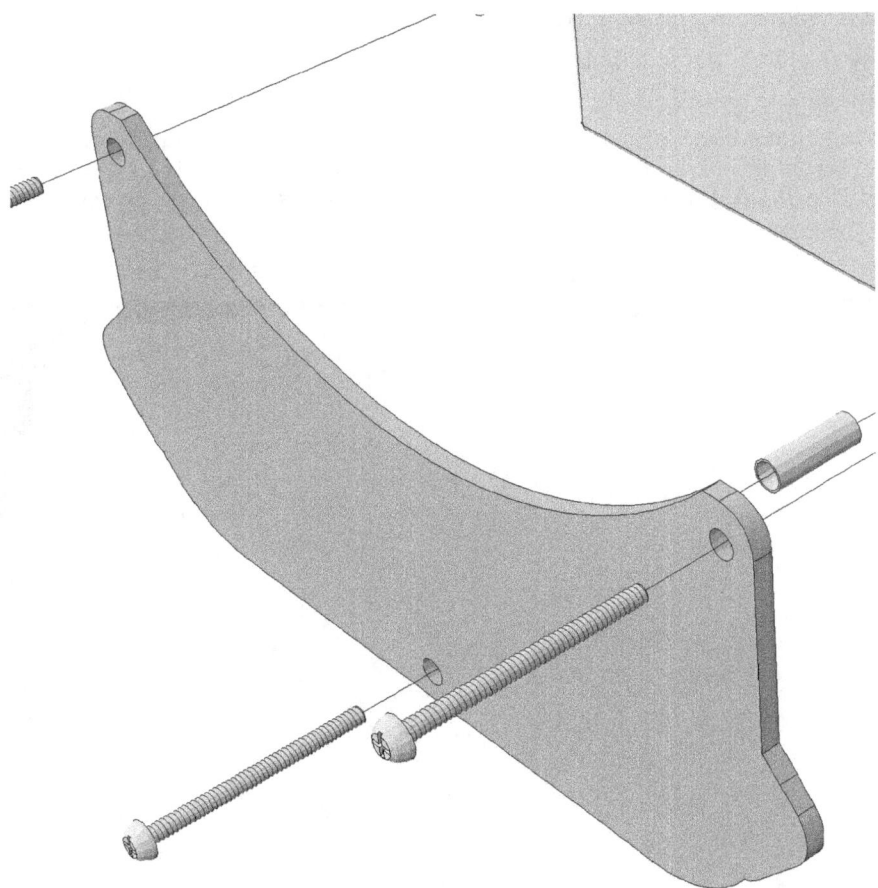

Figure 6.20

Tip

The vanity plate can be cut from thicker material. If so, you will need to use longer mounting screws when attaching it to the rear plate. For instance, if you make the plate out of 3/4" stock you will need to use at least 3-1/4" screws.

Conclusion

Appendix A contains two plate drawings. The drawings form the front plate and the rear plate. Depending on the size of the copier you are using, you may need to make an enlarged copy of the top and an enlarged copy of the bottom of a particlar plate and attach them together with tape to form a full size drawing as shown in Figure 6.21.

The easiest way to attach the sheets is to use a paper cutter or a pair of scissors to cut along the top line on the bottom half of the drawings. This makes it easy to align the sheets.

Once the drawings have been joined, you can use them to help with your design. Once you have cut the plates to your satisfaction, you may want to use a 1/8" round-over bit to round over all the edges. This is completely optional, but it may give your clock a more finished look. Some designs may look even better with crisp edges.

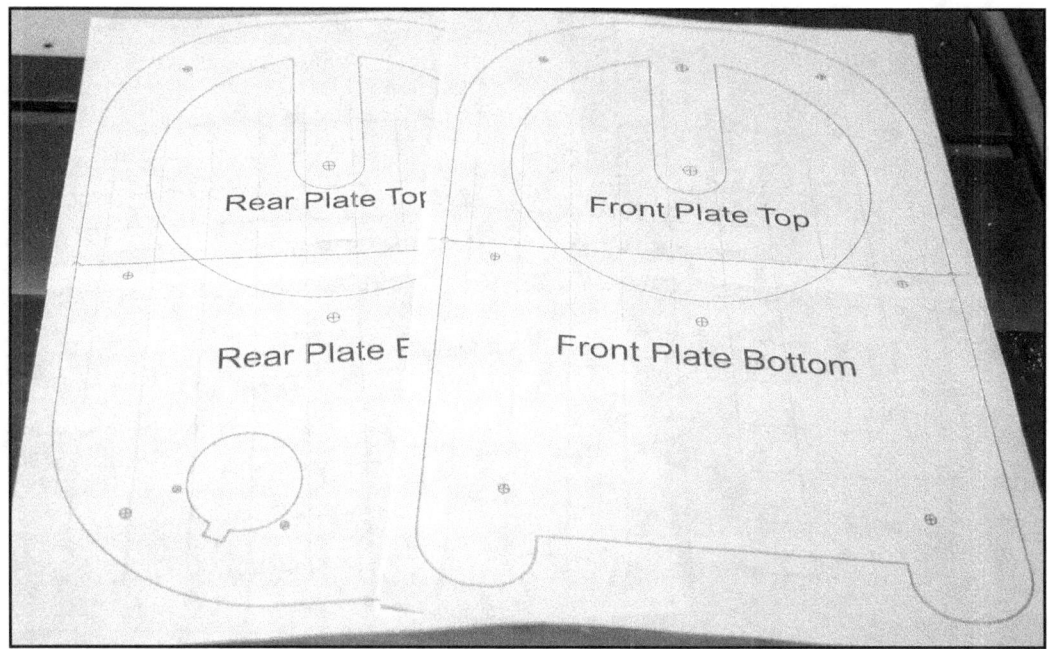

Figure 6.21

Tip

If you lay out and drill the holes in steps 1-4, you can align the individual drawing sheets with those holes in order to transfer any of the components. For example, you can align the rear bottom sheet with the four plate spacer holes, and mark the motor mount holes by using a center punch, as shown in Figure 6.22.

Figure 6.22

Chapter 7

Front Plate Assembly

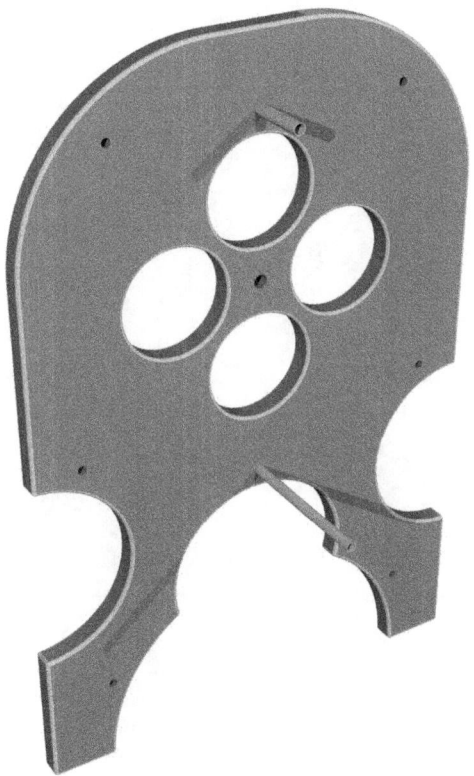

In order to attache the gears to the front plate, two arbors are permanently attached. These two arbors are also indexed into two holes on the rear plate. This is what keeps every thing lined up.

In this chapter you will also clean up the plates by sanding and routing the edges with a round-over bit.

Tools Needed For This Chapter

- Tubing cutter
- 120 Grit sandpaper
- Razor knife
- Metal file
- Mallet
- Thick CA wood glue
- 1/8" Drill bit

Components Needed For This Chapter

- 1/4" Brass tubing (single piece 1-5/8" long)
- 7/32" Brass tubing (single piece 3-5/8" long)

Prerequisites

The front and rear plates should have been cut.

Please note that while the drawings show the default HANS plate design, your design may vary. For example, the plates shown in Figure 7.1 were used during this chapter.

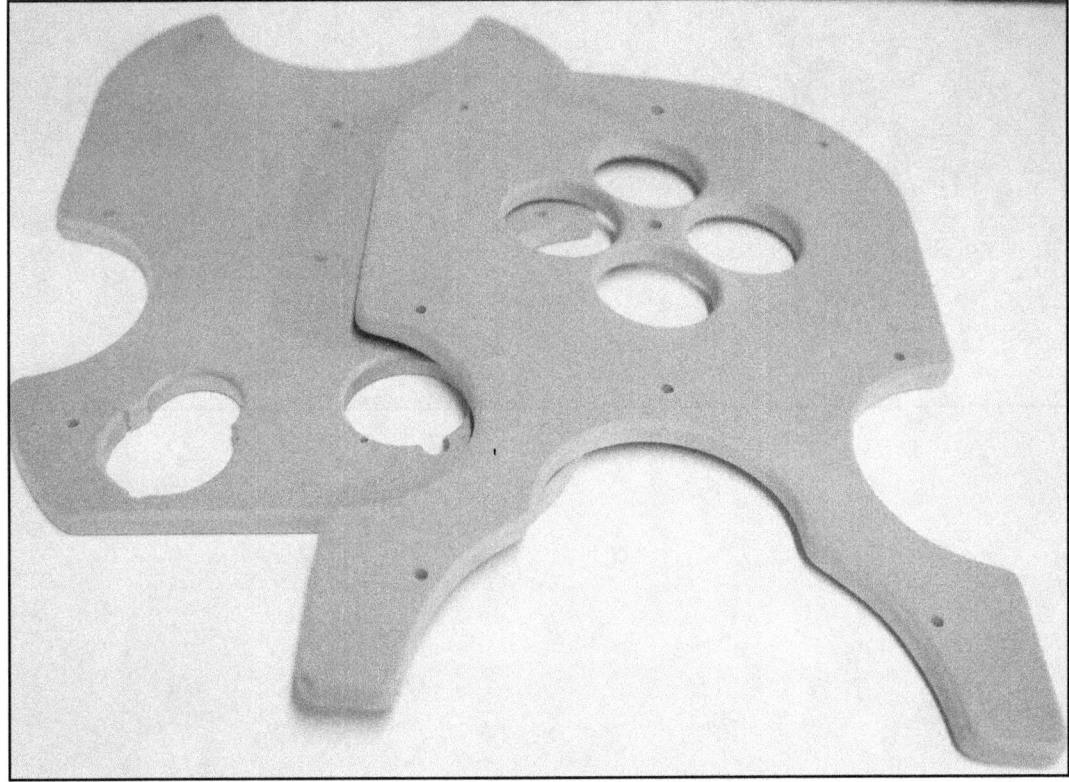

Figure 7.1

Step 1 - Final Touches to Clock Plates

Start by completely sanding the clock plates, paying particular attention to the edges. Figure 7.2 shows the rounded edges of a rear clock plate. If you have not rounded the edges of your plates yet, you may want to do that now, as you won't be able to do it later.

Remove all your marks from the stock; this will make it easier to finish later.

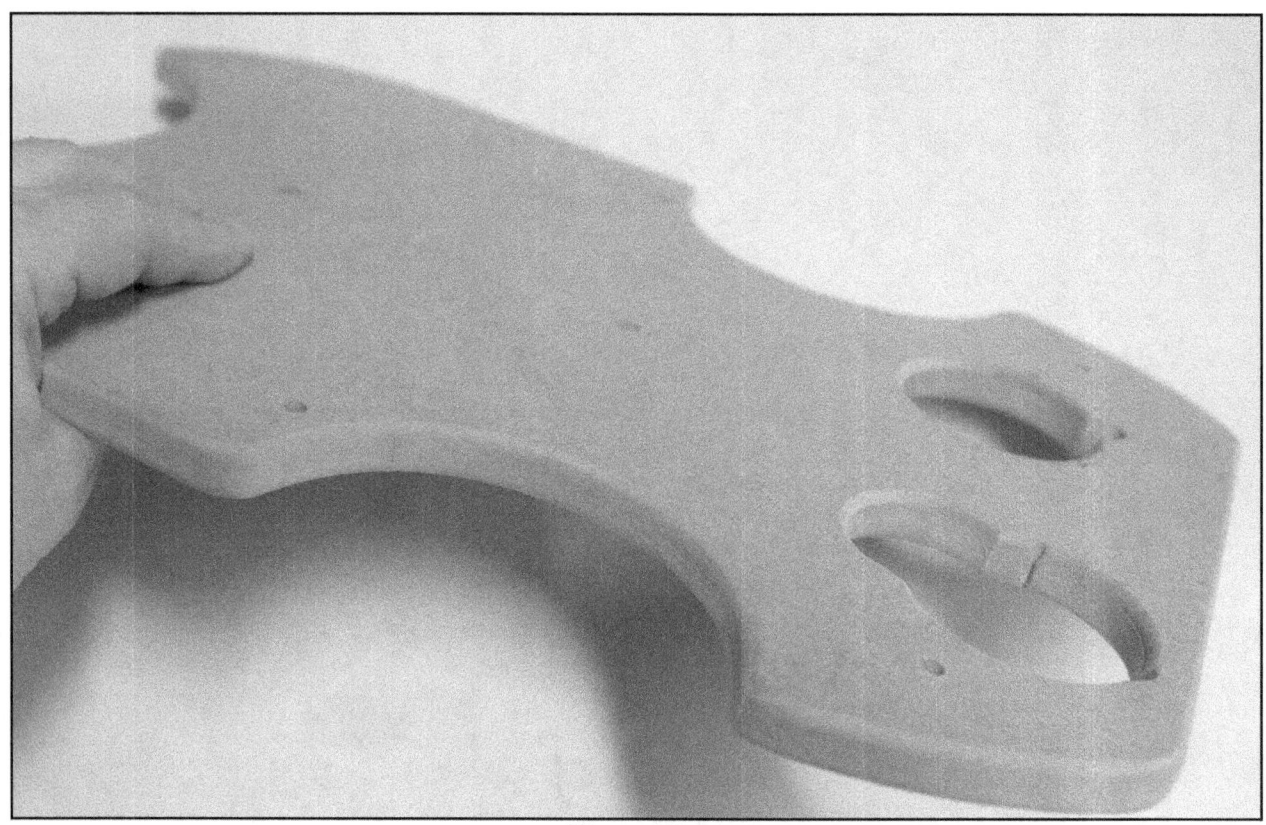

Figure 7.2

Step 2 - Gears 7 & 8 Arbor

Start by cutting a piece of 1/4" brass tubing to a length of 1-5/8". Clean the cut edges with a metal file and razor knife. Using the 120 grit sandpaper, rough up about 3/8" of one end. This will be the end you will insert into the clock plate.

Place a couple of drops of CA glue on the roughed up portion of the tube, then insert it into the 1/4" hole in the top center of the front clock plate as shown in Figure 7.3.

If the hole is too tight for the brass tube, use a wooden mallet or a piece of scrap and a hammer to gently tap it in place.

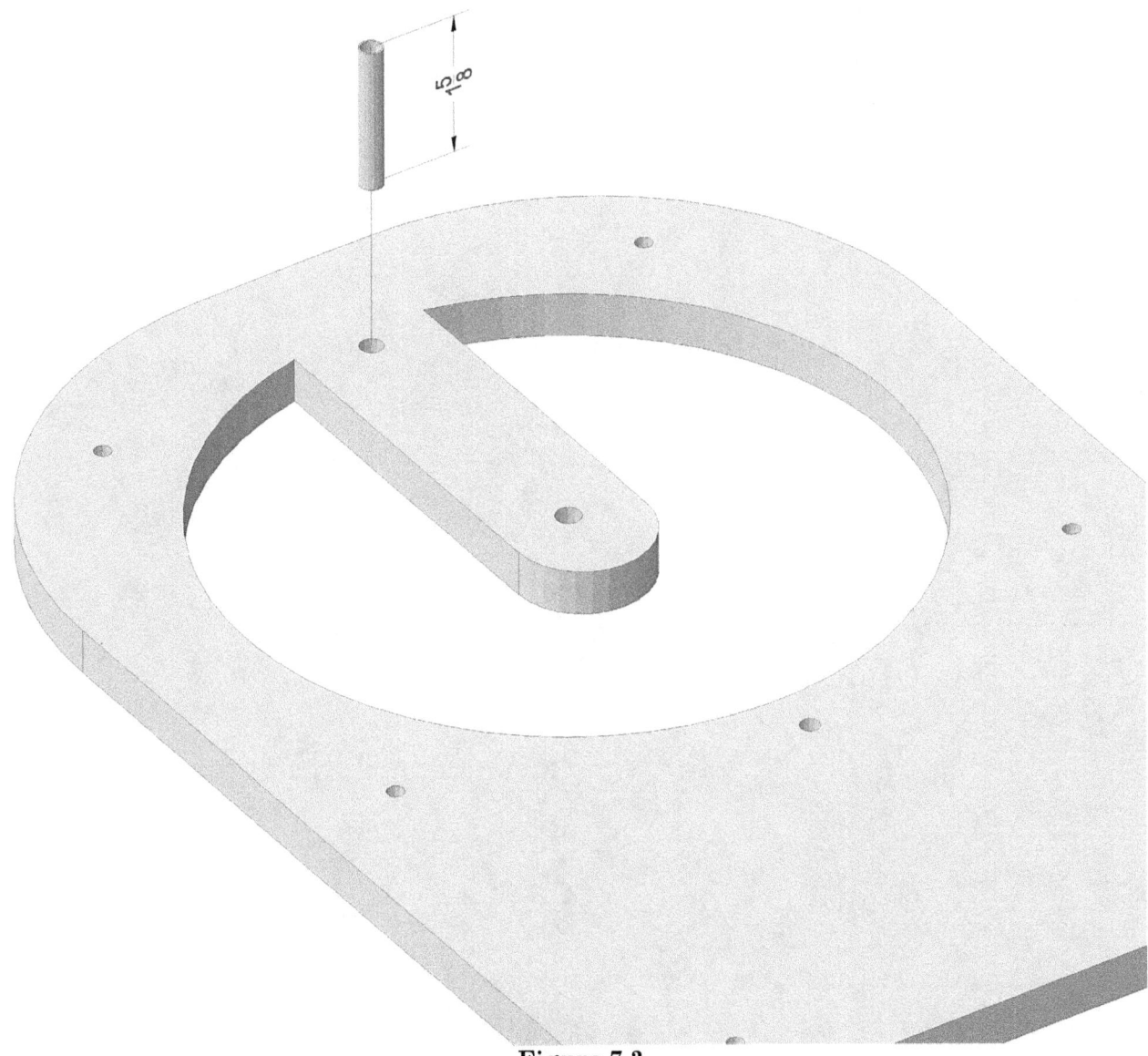

Figure 7.3

Step 3 - Gears 3 & 4 Arbor

Start by cutting a piece of 7/32" brass tubing to a length of 3-5/8". Clean the cut edges with a metal file and razor knife. Using the 120 grit sandpaper, rough up about 3/8" of one end. This will be the end you will insert into the clock plate.

Place a couple of drops of CA glue on the roughed up portion of the tube, then insert it into the 7/32" hole in the bottom center of the front clock plate as shown in Figure 7.4.

If the hole is too tight for the brass tube, use a wooden mallet or a piece of scrap and a hammer to gently tap it in place.

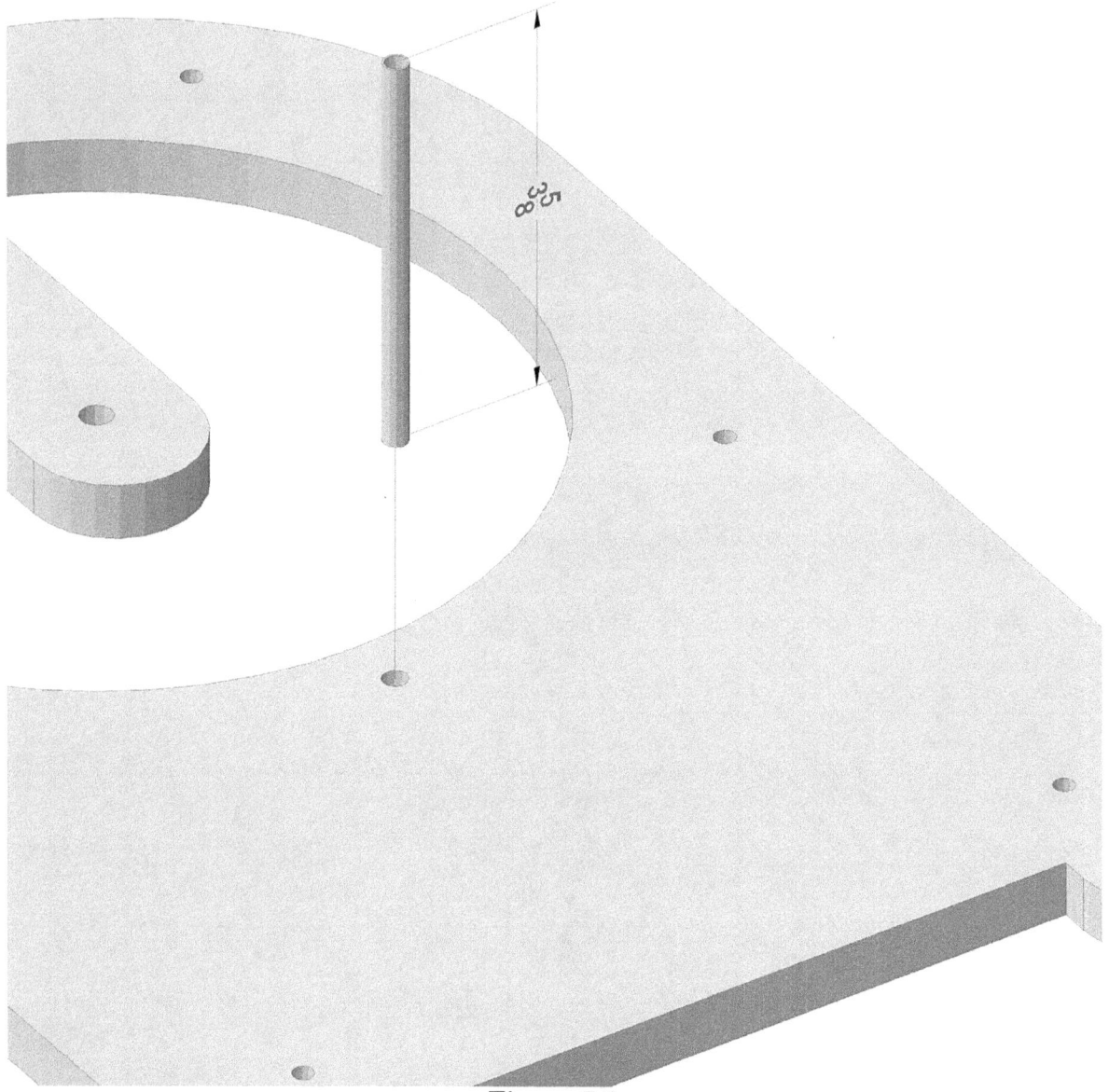

Figure 7.4

Step 4 - Let Glue Set

The final front plate should look something like the one shown in Figure 7.5, depending on your design variations. Set the front plate aside for a few hours to let the glue harden.

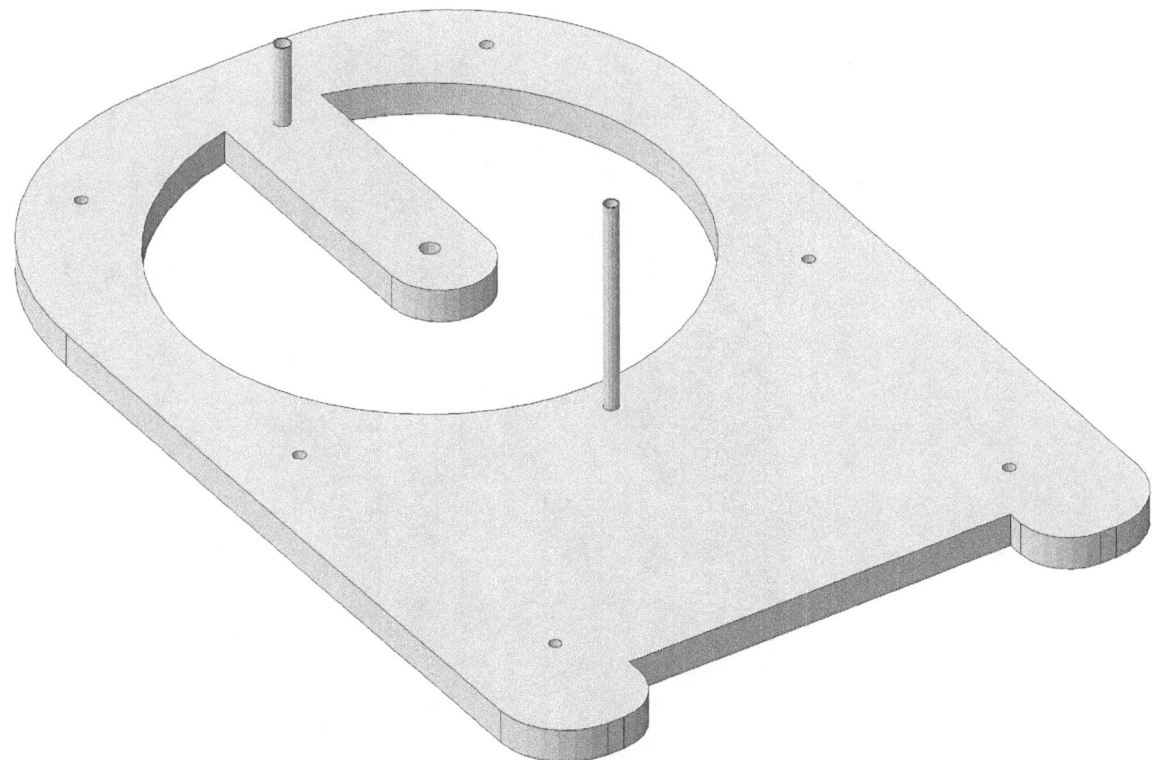

Figure 7.5

Conclusion

Your front plate may have just about any shape. However it will have a few things in common with any HANS style clock plate design. The arbors and mounting holes will all be the same, much like those shown in Figure 7.15. This is important, if later you don't like the look of your design you can simple create another and reuse your existing gears and motor.

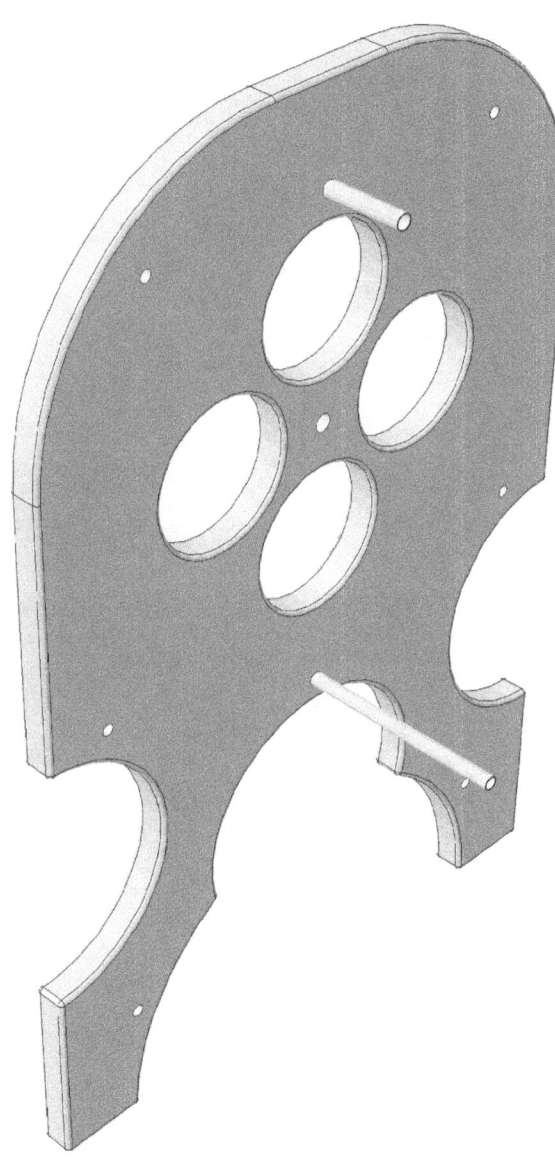

Figure 7.15

Chapter 8

Final Assembly

While this chapter is labeled "Final Assembly", in reality you need to think of it as pre assembly. You are going to completely assemble the clock, and once assembled make any adjustments or changes if a problem presents itself.

Later, you will disassemble the clock, apply your finish, and then reassemble the clock.

Tools Needed For This Chapter

- Tubing cutter
- 1/8" Drill bit
- 9/64" Drill bit
- 3/16" Drill bit
- Power drill or drill press
- Phillips screwdriver

Components Needed For This Chapter

- 12, #6 x 1-14" Brass wood screws
- Synchron clock motor
- 2, #6-32 x 1/2" Machine screws
- Power cord
- 2, Wire connectors (screw on type)
- 1/4" Plastic cable clamp
- 1, #8 x 1/2" pan head wood screw
- 3, #6-32 x 1-1/2" machine screws
- 3, #6-32 Hex nuts
- 9/32 Brass tubing
- 9, 7/32" Thin spacers
- 1, 9/32" Thin spacer
- 5, 1/4" Thin spacer
- 1, Locking spacer
- 2, 7/32" Thick spacers

Prerequisites

The front, rear, and vanity plates should have been completed. All other parts should have been cut and readily available. All sub assemblies outlined in previous chapters should have been completed.

You should have purchased your motor, but if not, the Synchron clock motor can be purchased from Timesavers, part number 18404. Timesavers is located at www.timesavers.com.

The motor also can be found at:

http://www.clock-parts.com/catalogmain2.asp?GroupID=211&Level=4

For the power cord, purchase a standard two-conductor extension cord, then cut the female end off and strip the wires.

Please note that while the drawings show the default HANS plate design, your design may vary.

Step 1 - Attach the Clock Face

Orient the clock face so that the XII numeral is at the top, as shown in Figure 8.1. Slip four #6 x 1-1/4" brass wood screws into the clock face mounting holes. Slip a 7/32" thin spacer onto the screws, then pass the screws into the plate mounting holes as shown in Figure 8.1.

Use four of the plate spacers like nuts and tighten them on the four screws. Insert two #6 x 1-1/4" brass screws into the lower two plate mounting holes. Using two plate spacers, tighten them on the screws.

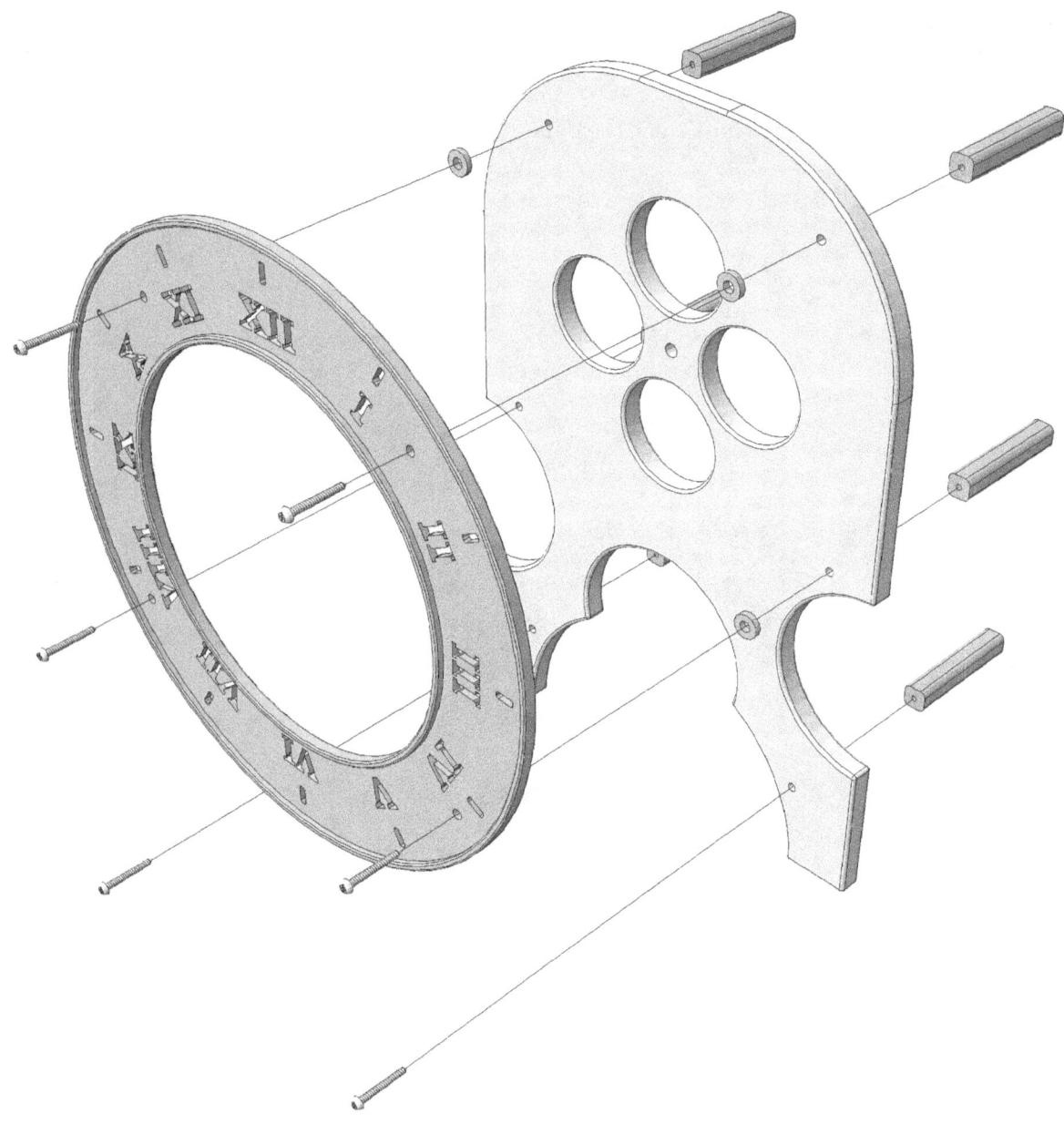

Figure 8.1

The finished assembly should look like the one shown in Figure 8.2.

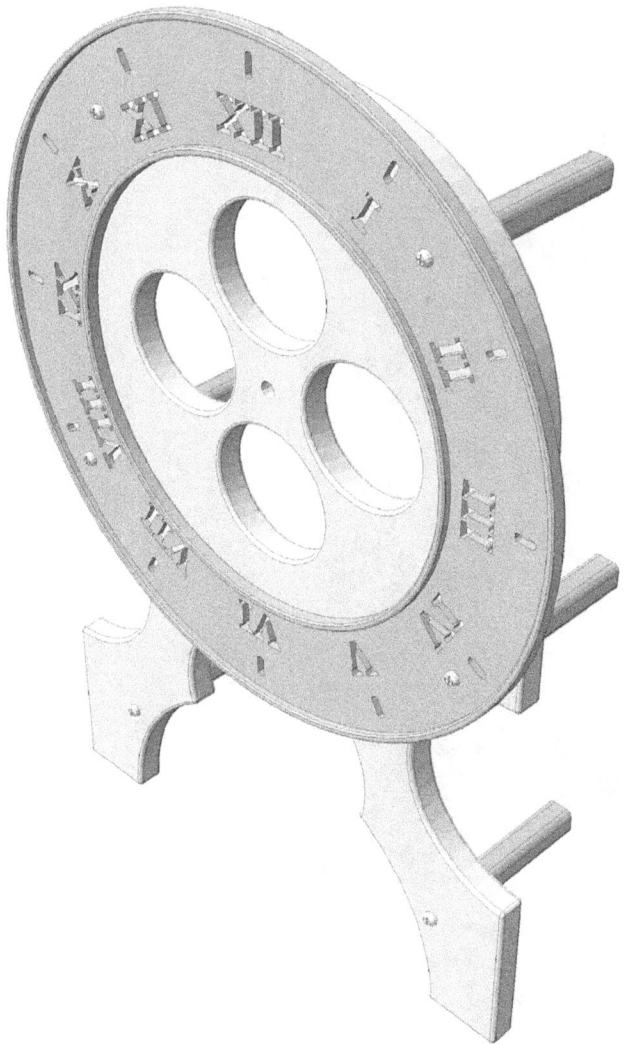

Figure 8.2

Tip

It may be easier to attach the face using one screw at a time. To do this, attach one screw as outlined, but leave it loose. Move to the next screw, lifting the face and slipping the spacer between the face and plate, then insert the screw. Repeat for the two remaining screws.

Step 2 - Attach Gear 9

Take the gear 9 assembly and insert a 9/32" thin spacer onto the arbor, then slip the arbor into the center hole of the clock plate as shown in Figure 8.3.

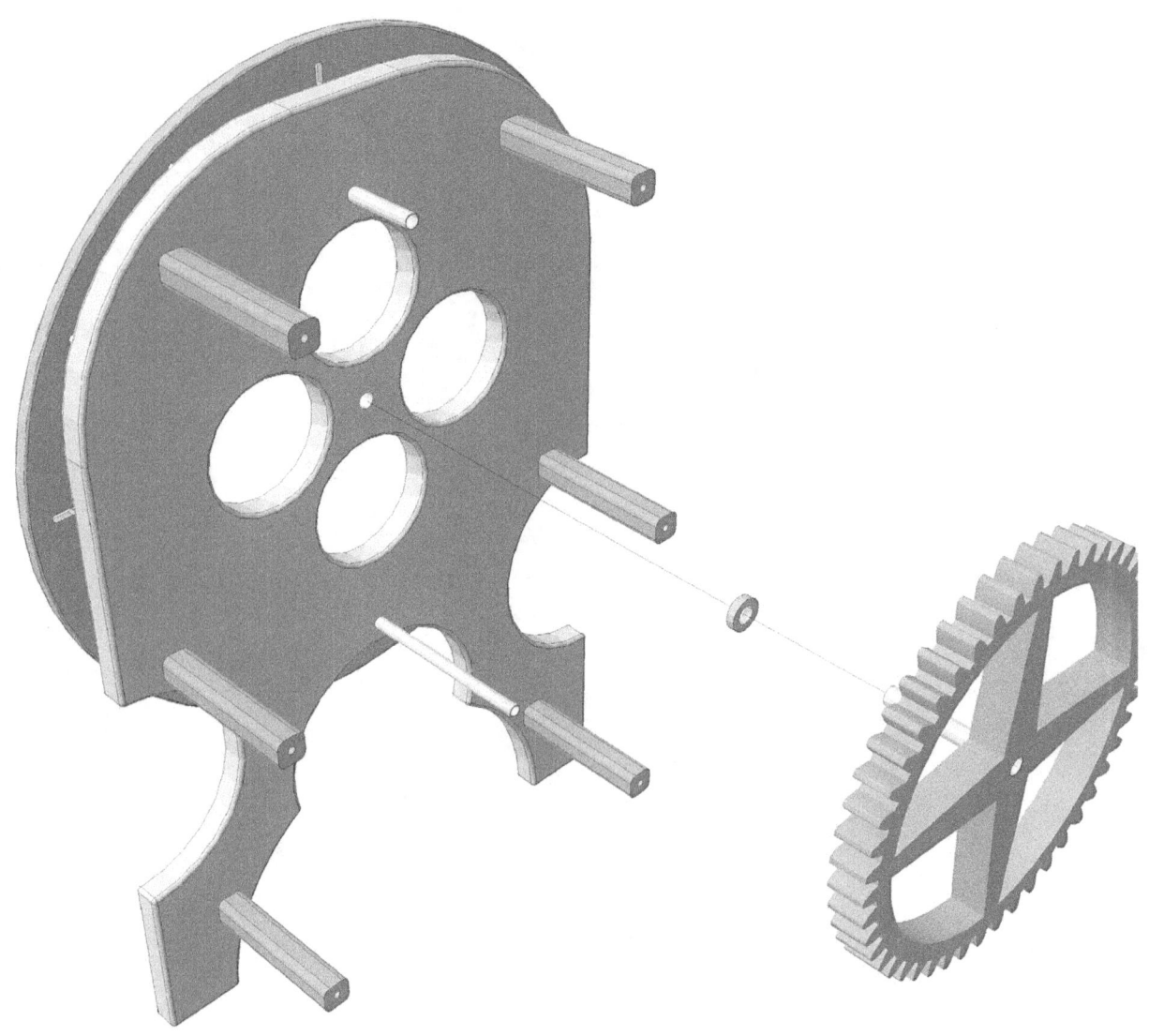

Figure 8.3

Step 3 - Attach Gears 7 and 8

Slip a 1/4" thin spacer over the top arbor as shown in Figure 8.4. Then, take the 7 and 8 gear assembly and insert it on the 1/4" top arbor, as shown in Figure 8.4.

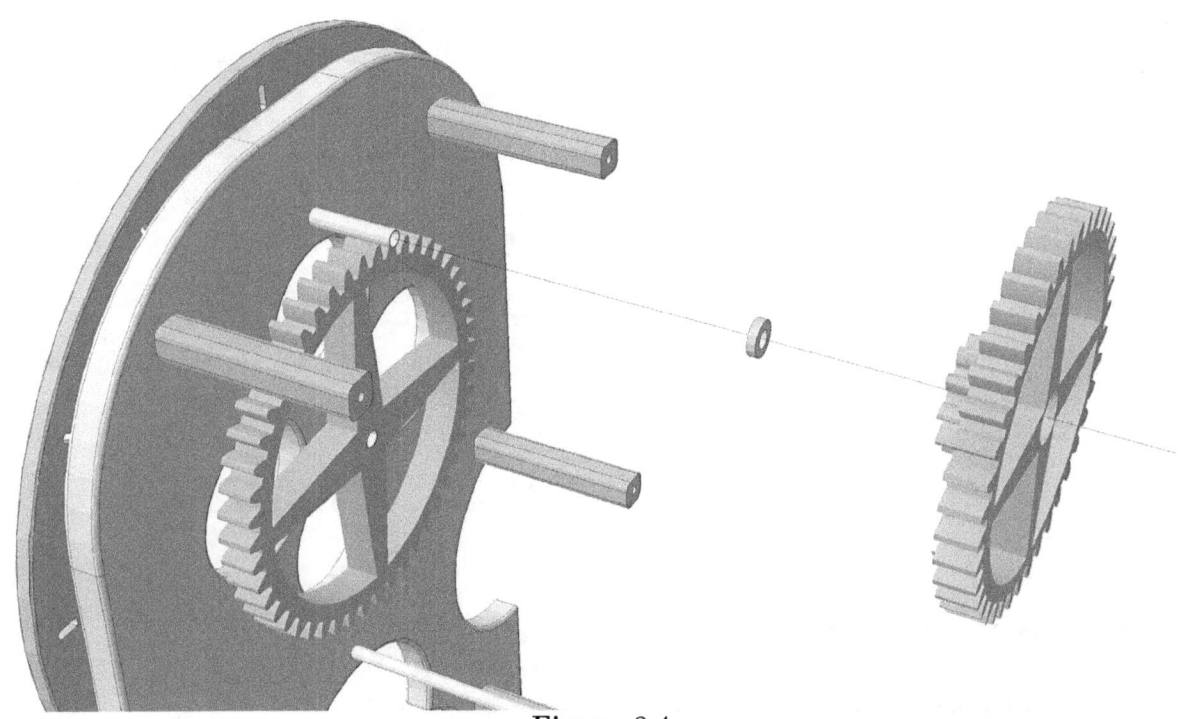

Figure 8.4

Step 4 - Add Locking Spacer

Slip the locking spacer (thin spacer #16) onto the top arbor as shown in Figure 8.5. The locking spacer holds the 7 and 8 gear assembly in place.

The lock should be tight enough to keep the gears from slipping off, but loose enough to allow the gears to spin freely.

Figure 8.5

Step 5 - Add Thick Gear Spacers

Take the two 7/32" thick gear spacers and add them to the lower 7/32" arbor, as shown in Figure 8.6.

These are referenced as thick spacers 1 and 2 in the drawings.

Figure 8.6

Step 6 - Attach Gears 5 and 6

Slip a 1/4" thin spacer over the arbor on the end nearest the smaller gear, as shown in Figure 8.7. Take the 5 and 6 gear assembly and insert it into the gear 9 arbor, as shown in Figure 8.7.

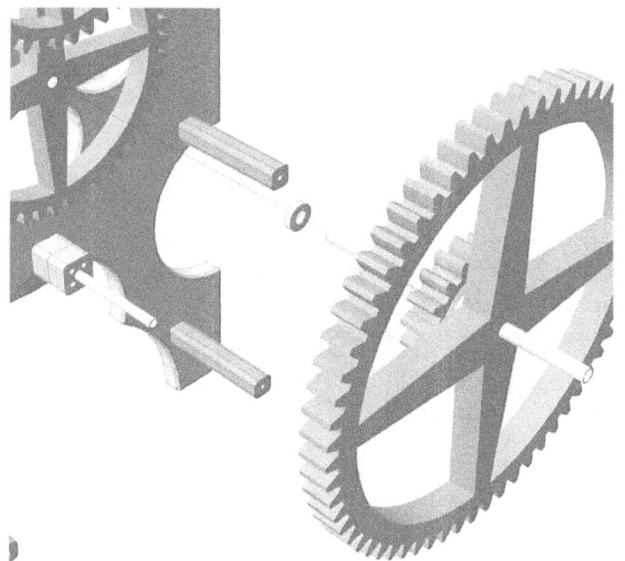

Figure 8.7

88   *Chapter 8*   Final Assembly

Step 7 - Add Thin Spacers to Lower Arbor

Slip three 7/32" thin spacers over the lower 7/32" arbor as shown in Figure 8.8.

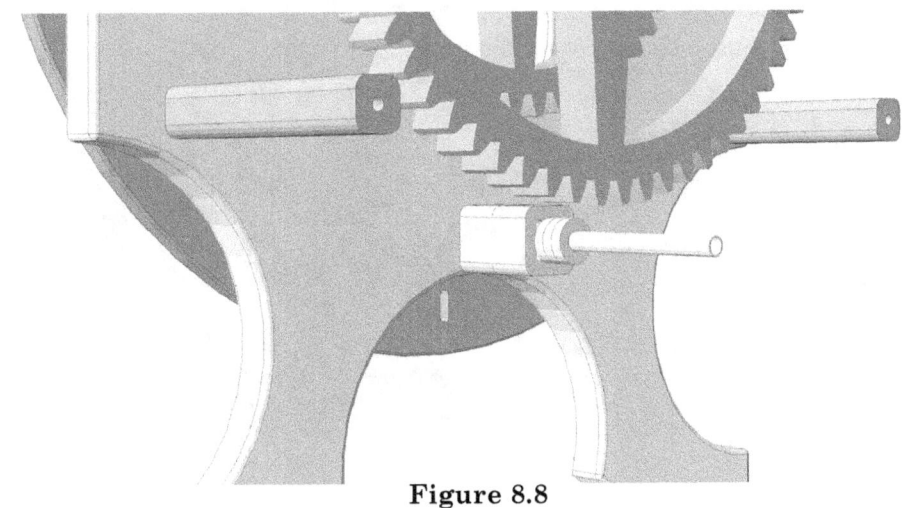

Figure 8.8

Step 8 - Attach Gears 3 and 4

Slip the 3 and 4 gear assembly onto the lower 7/32" arbor as shown in Figure 8.9.

Figure 8.9

Step 9 - Add Thick Gear Spacer

Take the thick spacer with a 1/4" center hole and add it to the 1/4" arbor on the 5 and 6 gear assembly, as shown in Figure 8.10.

This are referenced as thick spacers 3 in the drawings.

Figure 8.10

Step 10 - Add Remaining Thin Spacers

Slip three thin spacers with 1/4" center holes over the 1/4" arbor as shown in Figure 8.11.

Next, slip two thin spacers with 7/32" center holes over the 7/32" arbor.

Figure 8.11

Step 11 - Attach the Rear Plate

Take the rear plate and position it over the 1/4" center and 7/32" lower arbors. Once positioned, insert the six #6 x 1-1/4" brass wood screws into the six mounting holes, as shown in Figure 8.12.

With the rear plate now attached to the front plate, you should be able to freely rotate the gears. Spin gear 3 with your fingers; it should spin freely. If doesn't try loosening the six wood screws and with the rear plate once again loose try spinning it again. If gears now spin, the plate is too snug against the gears when the screws are tightened. Don't panic, this is common.

To remedy the problem, remove the plate and remove one of the 1/4" thin spacers and one of the 7/32" thin spacers that you added in Step 10. Holding the spacers with your fingers, rub them against some 120 grit sandpaper to reduce the thickness.

Once thinned, add the spacers back and reattach the plate. If it is still too tight, go back and remove more material from the spacers.

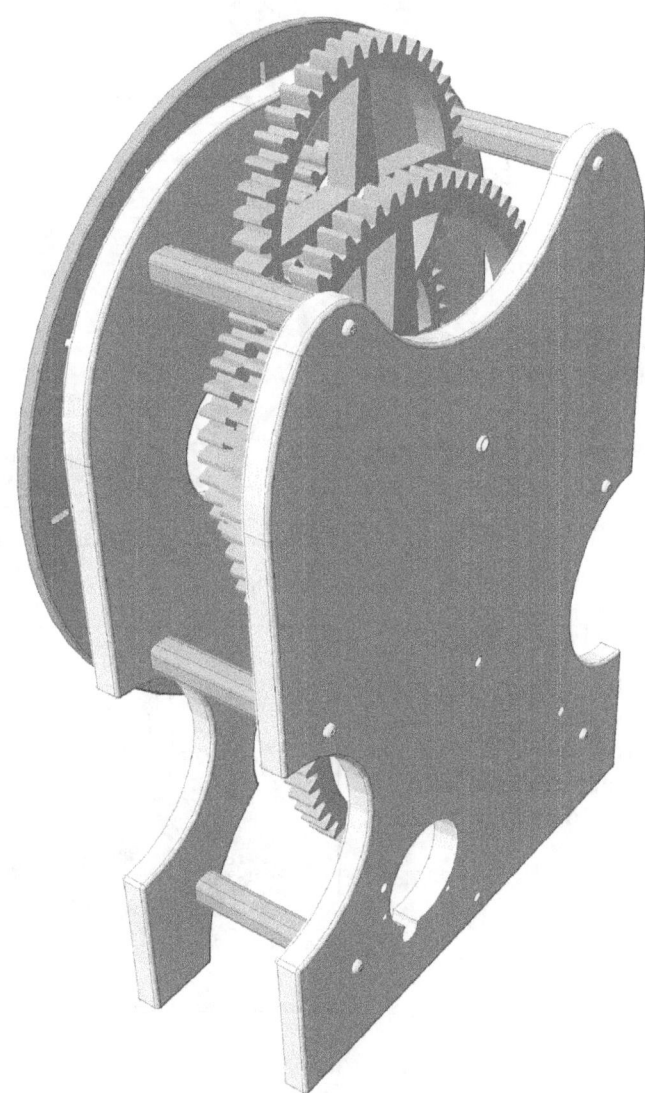

Figure 8.12

Step 12 - Prepare the Motor

Once you have the gears moving smoothly, you need to remove the rear plate and attach the motor.

Using a portable drill or drill press, widen the holes of the two larger tabs to 9/64", as shown in Figure 8.13.

Figure 8.13

Step 13 - Attach Motor to Rear Plate

If you have not done so yet, remove the rear plate from the clock.

Using two #6-32 x 1/2" machine screws, attach the motor to the rear plate as shown in Figure 8.14.

Do not over tighten the screws or you will strip the holes.

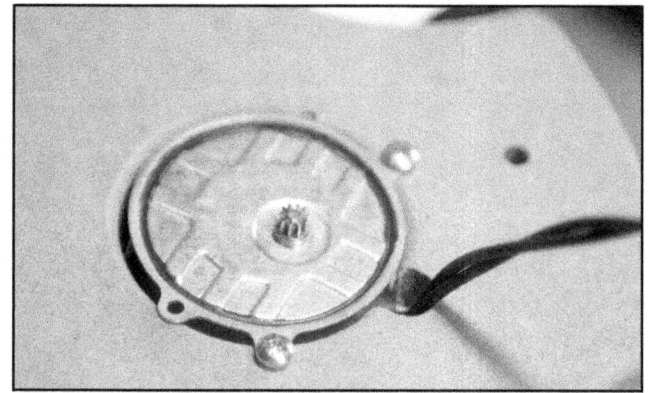

Figure 8.14

Step 14 - Attach Drive Gear

The drive gear has a 3/16" center hole. This hole is a little smaller than the gear attached to the motor. By pressing the center hole on the driver gear firmly over the small metal gear on the motor, you should be able to snap it in place, as shown in Figure 8.15.

Figure 8.15

As an alternative, the Kronos Robotics spacer pack comes with a gear spacer designed to fit perfectly over the motor gear.

Using yellow wood glue, glue the drive gear spacer to the drive gear, as shown in Figure 8.16.

Once the glue has dried (about 30 minutes), slip the gear spacer over the metal gear attached to the motor, as shown in Figure 8.17. It is a tight fit so proceed carefully. An easy way to do it is to hold the drive gear at an angle so that one of the teeth on the motor gear seats in the gear spacer. Once indexed, press firmly.

Once the drive gear is attached, do not remove it.

Figure 8.16

Figure 8.17

Building the Hans Electric Gear Clock

Step 15 - Wire the Motor

The quickest and easiest way to wire the motor, is to use two wire connectors. Start by twisting together one of the wires on your power cord together with one of the clock motor wires. Then take one of the wire connectors and screw it over the twisted wire, as shown in Figure 8.18. Repeat with the other power cord wire, motor wire, and connector.

Next, secure the wires with a 1/4" cable clamp and #8 x 1/2" wood screw. It is important that you fill the clamp with wires so that they are held snugly. This can be done by folding the cable back and including both the motor wires and power cord, as shown in Figure 8.19.

The clamp should be attached to the plate near the center at about 1-1/4" above the center vanity plate hole, as shown in Figure 8.19.

If you created both motor mounting holes, you can route the cord through the unused hole and out the back. If not, the cable can be routed out the side of the clock.

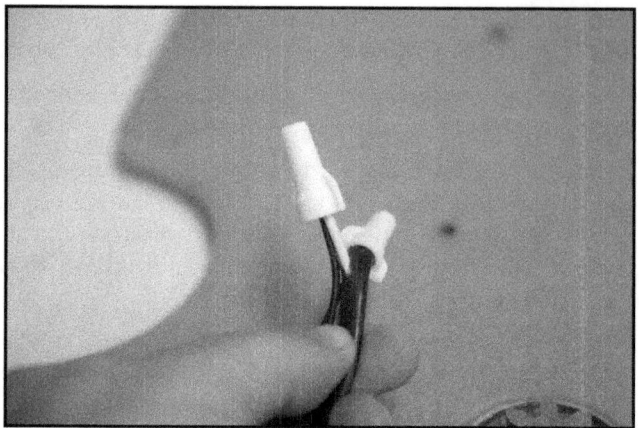

Figure 8.18

Figure 8.19

Step 16 - Attach Vanity Plate

Cut three pieces of 9/32" tubing to a length of 3/4". Insert the machines screws into the holes in the vanity plate, then through the spacer, and finally through the rear plate, as shown in Figure 8.20.

Attach three #6-32 hex nuts to the screws.

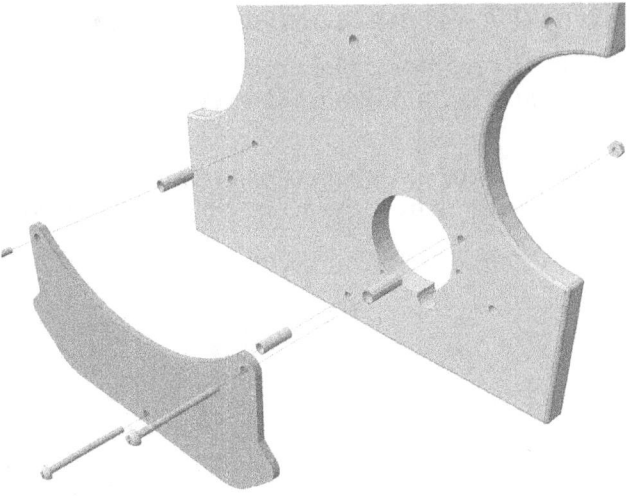

Figure 8.20

The finished plate assembly should like those shown in Figure 8.21.

Figure 8.21

Step 17 - Re-attach the Rear Plate

Take the rear plate and position it over the 1/4" center and 7/32" lower arbors. Once positioned, use the six #6 x 1-1/4" brass wood screws and insert them into the six mounting holes, as shown in Figure 8.22.

Note that the gears cannot be turned manually once the motor is installed. If you force them you may strip the arbors from the gears. You should however have some play in the gears.

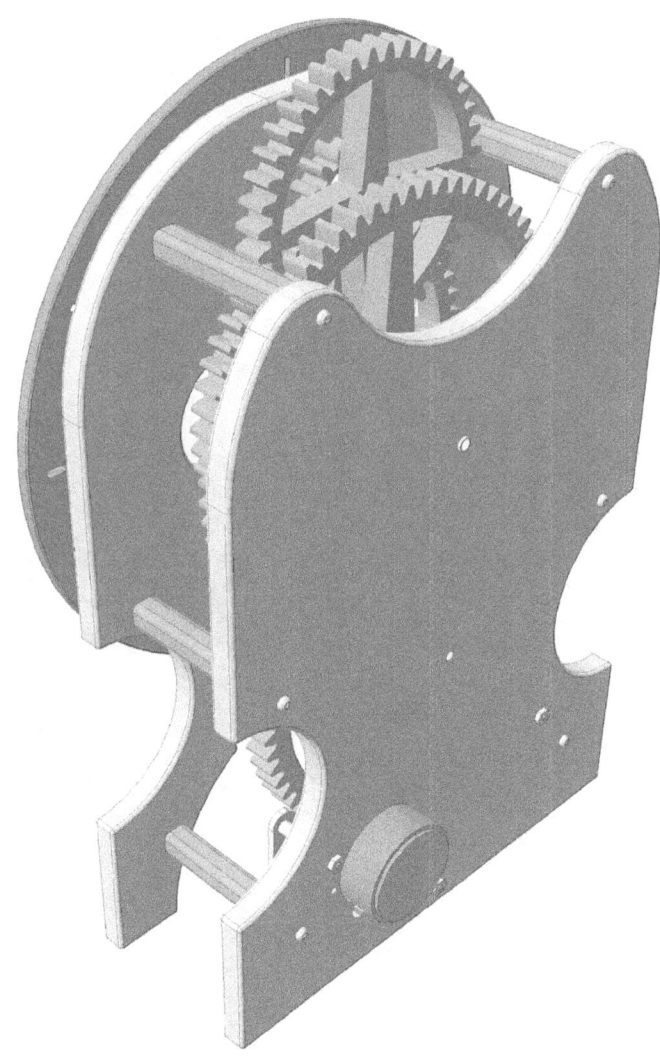

Figure 8.22

Step 18 - Attach Hour Hand

Take the hour hand and insert it onto the inner arbor as shown in 8.23.

Figure 8.23

Step 19 - Assemble the Minute Hand

The minute hand consists of three components, the hand and two small spacers that create a cap to cover the brass arbors.

First, glue the two small 1/2" spacers together. One of the spacers has a 1/4" hole, while the other is solid. When the glue is dry, glue them both to the minute hand as shown in 8.24.

Use a small piece of 1/4" scrap tubing to align the cap with the hole in the hand.

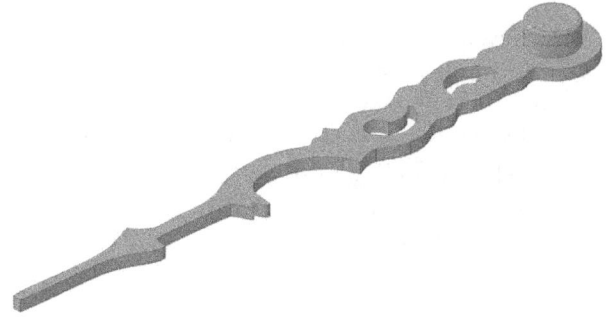

Figure 8.24

Step 18 - Attach Minute Hand

Take the minute hand assembly and insert it onto the outer arbor as shown in 8.25.

Step 19 - Test the Clock

Plug the clock's power cord into an AC outlet and set the time by moving each of the hands shown in 8.25.

Let the clock run for several hours to make sure it's running properly. The time should remain near perfect. If it does not, then it's possible the gears are providing too much back pressure for the motor.

If this happens, you will have to remove the rear plate and re-test the gears to make sure they are running smoothly.

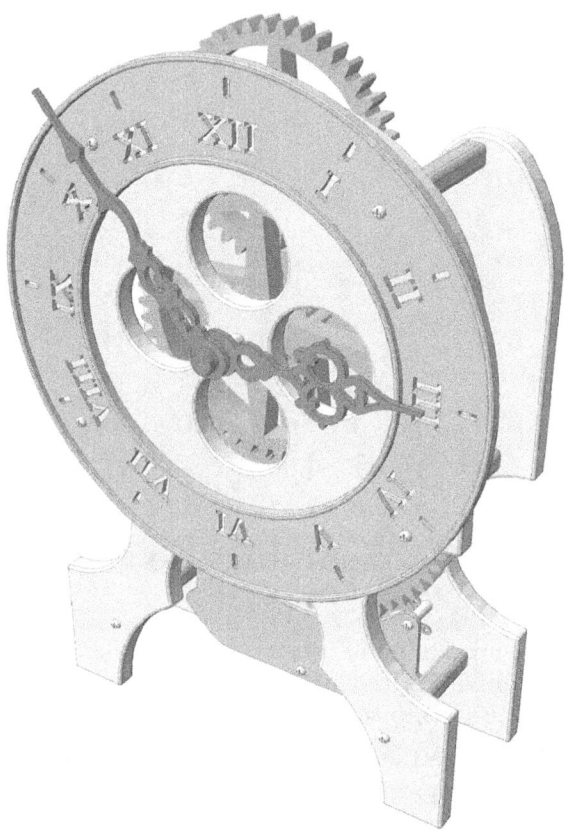

Figure 8.25

Chapter 9

Finishing The Clock

Choosing the colors and finishing effects is the next step in determining your clock's personality. This chapter will take you through the finishing process used to create some great antiquing effects that will make your clock look aged.

The various sections of the clock will be finished separately as they will use slightly different techniques. For instance, the clock plates, vanity plate, and clock plate spacers are all done using the same technique and colors. The gear assemblies use different techniques and colors. While these are shown separately, you can do one while the other is drying.

Tools Needed For This Chapter

- Phillips screwdriver (to disassemble the clock)
- Foam brushes
- Extra fine sanding sponge
- 400 Grit sandpaper

While you can use 400 grit sanding paper throughout the finishing process, the sanding sponges are easier to use on the flat surfaces and straight edges. You can also wash the sanding sponges for re-use.

Components Needed For This Chapter

- Generals Brick-Red milk paint
- Generals Somerset Gold milk paint
- Generals Outback Brown milk paint
- Generals Pitch Black glaze
- Acrylic paint, flat black
- Acrylic paint, gold

The colors shown above are just suggestions, Feel free to try other combinations of colors and techniques.

Prerequisites

The clock should have been assembled and tested. Before applying the finish you need to disassemble the clock.

Note, do not disassemble items that have been glued. Remove the motor from the rear plate, but don't remove the drive gear from the motor.

During this chapter, the effects will be shown using the design shown in Figure 9.1. If you used the default design or one of your own the processes shown will be the same.

Figure 9.1

Finishing the Clock Plates

Step 1 - Apply Highlight Color

If you want to utilize a highlight on the plate edges, apply it now to all the edges as shown in Figure 9.2. The highlight shown here is Generals milk paint "Somerset Gold".

After the first coat dries, sand thoroughly with the sanding sponge. Apply three more coats, sanding only lightly after each coat dries.

You need to apply the highlight color to the front plate, rear plate, vanity plate, and the clock plate spacers.

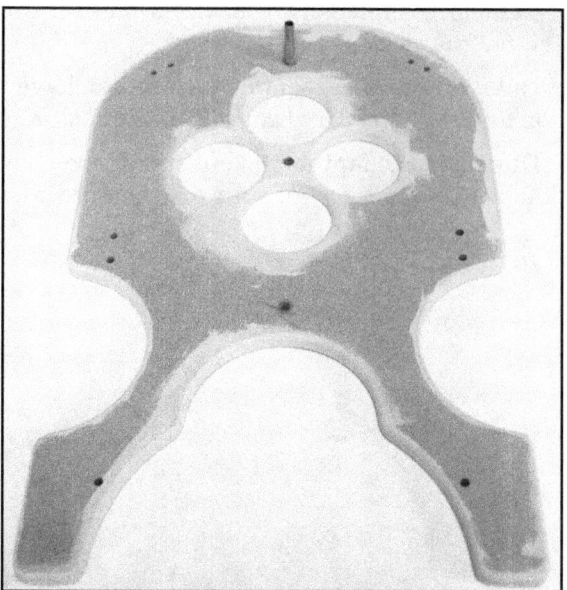

Figure 9.2

Step 2 - Apply Main Color

Apply the main color to the plates, as shown in Figure 9.3. Do one side, let it dry, then do the other. Don't forget all the edges. The main color shown here is Generals milk paint "Outback Brown".

After the first coat on all surfaces is dry, thoroughly sand with a sanding sponge. Apply three or four more coats, sanding only lightly after each coat dries.

You need to apply the main color to the front plate, rear plate, vanity plate, and the clock plate spacers.

You need to also paint the thick spacers with the same color.

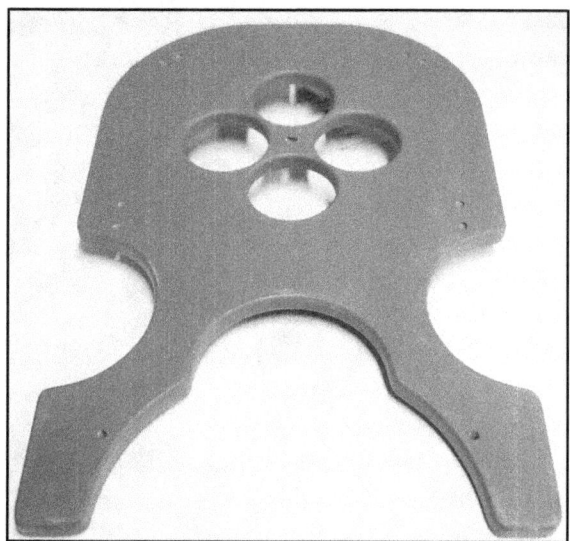

Figure 9.3

Tip

The highlight color will show through the main color, even after several coats. It is ok to be a little sloppy as it will add to the effect later.

Step 3 - Apply Glaze

Apply the glaze to the plates as shown in Figure 9.4. The glaze is applied with a foam brush, then removed with a shop towel or rag. When you remove the glaze, swipe the length of the plate. This will create a dark grain effect.

Do one side, let it dry, then do the other. Once both sides are complete, apply the glaze to the edge but don't wipe it off. The glaze shown here is Generals "Pitch Black".

You need to apply the glaze to the front plate, rear plate, vanity plate, and the clock plate spacers.

You also need to apply glaze to the thick spacers.

Note that only one coat of glaze is used.

Figure 9.4

Step 4 - Sand Corners to Reveal Highlights

Take the sanding sponge and start sanding the corners of all edges to reveal the highlight color, as shown in Figure 9.5. Be careful not to sand too much or you will sand through the highlight down to the stock.

If the sanding sponge gets loaded, it will become ineffective. When this happens, wash the sponge and let it dry.

Figure 9.5

Tip

The inside arcs can present a problem for the sanding sponge. For these, you can sometimes purchase rounded sanding sponges. You can also wrap some 400 grit paper around a pencil or dowel and use that to sand the inside arcs.

The finished front plate should look like the one shown in Figure 9.6.

Figure 9.6

Finishing the Gears

Step 1 - Apply Main Color

Apply the main color to the gears as shown in Figure 9.7. Do the teeth first by dipping the foam brush into the paint and forcing it between the teeth. You can do several teeth with each dip. Be sure to coat all the teeth, but don't leave excess paint as it could effect the performance of the gears.

Once the teeth are done, coat the rest of the clock. Be sure to get the foam brush in between the larger and smaller gears.

The paint shown here is Generals milk paint "Brick Red".

After the first coat on all surfaces is dry, thoroughly sand with a sanding sponge. You don't need to sand the gear teeth. The gears only need two coats.

Figure 9.7

Tip

Try to get as little paint as possible on the brass tubing. It must be cleaned off later before resembling the clock.

When painting the gears, be sure to apply enough paint to fill the small holes. Its fine of they are not filled completely. When you apply the glaze later, it will settle in the hole and help with the effect.

Building the Hans Electric Gear Clock   **105**

Step 2 - Apply Glaze

Apply the glaze to the gears, as shown in Figure 9.8. The glaze is applied with a foam brush, then removed with a shop towel or rag.

Do the teeth first, much like you did when applying the paint. Once the teeth are coated, move to the face opposite the small gear and quickly coat it, then wipe off the excess. Be sure the glaze gets into the small holes. Next glaze the opposite face; be sure to get in between the small gear and large gear.

Tip

When glazing, hold the gear assembly by the smaller gear. You can come back to the small gear later after the main gear is finished.

When doing the teeth, you don't need to wipe off the excess. Just let it dry.

If you want the gears to appear darker, repeat the process, once the glaze has dried.

Finish the gear by glazing the inside cutouts of the gear. Be sure to get the glaze in the corners, then wipe off the excess. The glaze shown here is Generals "Pitch Black".

Figure 9.8

106 *Chapter 9* Finishing The Clock

Finishing the Face

Step 1 - Apply Under Coat

Apply the under coat to the face, as shown in Figure 9.9. This will take about five coats. Be sure to sand thoroughly after the first coat, then lightly between coats.

The paint shown here is Generals milk paint "Somerset Gold".

The goal here is to cover the original color of the stock used to make the face.

Figure 9.9

You will be applying gold acrylic paint to the face. By using a lighter color, the gold finish will appear brighter. If you use an undercoating of black acrylic before applying the final gold color, the face will be much darker and take on the appearance of an antique.

Keep in mind that the hands will be dark. You may want some contrast between the hands and face. With a dark face, brighten the hands.

Step 2 - Apply Main Color

Apply the main color to the face, as shown in Figure 9.10. This will take three or four coats. Sand only lightly between coats.

The paint shown here is a simple acrylic gold, found at most craft stores.

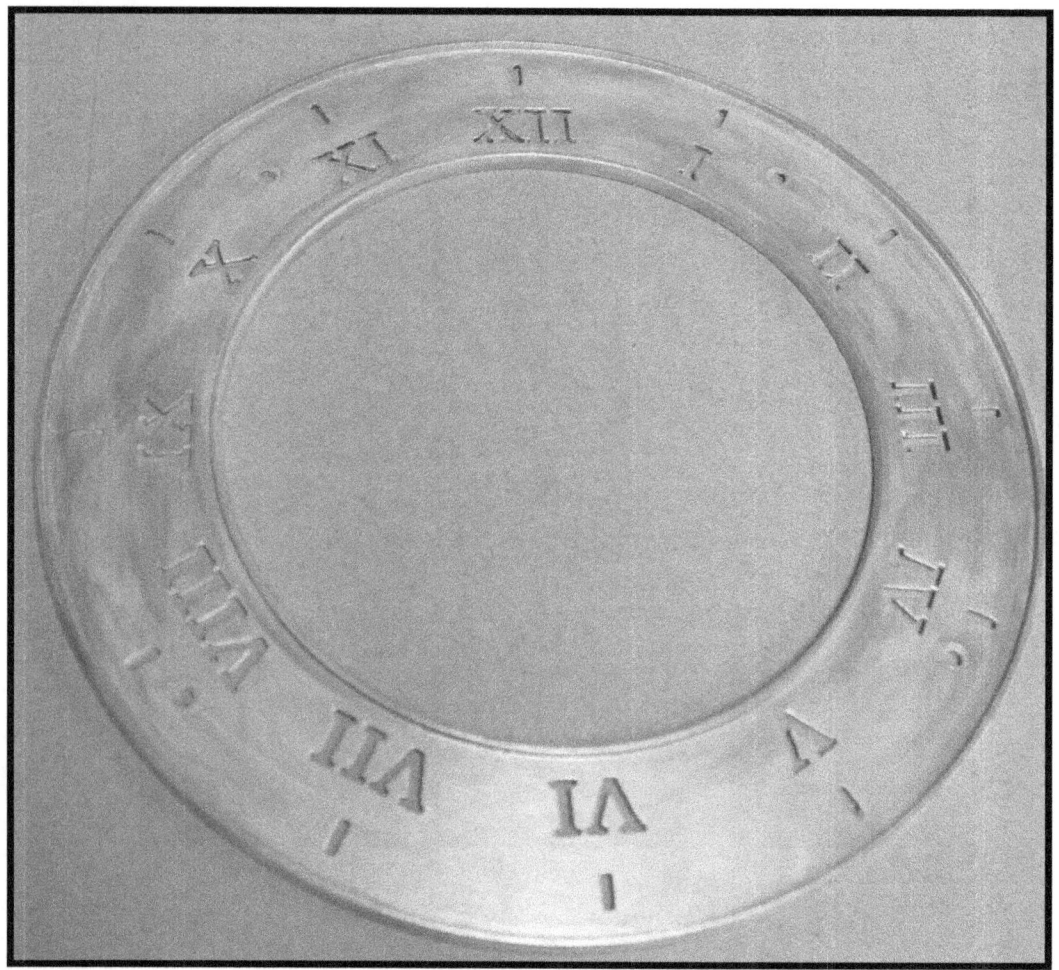

Figure 9.10

Clock Hands

Step 1 - Paint the Hands

Using black acrylic, paint the hands, as shown in Figure 9.11. A single coat will do it.

As an option, you can apply a very thin coat of acrylic gold paint to the hands for a slightly antique metal look.

Figure 9.11

Finishing Other Parts

You may want to paint the drive gear. Paint in place, but don't remove it from the motor. The acrylic black is a good color for the gear. You can also apply a thin coat of the acrylic black to the front and back of the motor. This will help the motor blend into the clock.

If you went with a different color scheme, apply the appropriate color to the motor. It is better if the motor blends in than is shown in contrast.

Reassemble the Clock

Using the instructions in the last chapter, reassemble the clock. Be sure to assemble in the same order as directed so that you can test the gear mesh. If you find that the gears jam, it is probably because you have glob of paint inside one of the teeth. Use a razor knife to remove it. Once the test is complete, proceed with the assembly.

Be careful when attaching the screws as you can mar the surface if your screwdriver slips.

Figure 9.12

Chapter 10

Conclusion

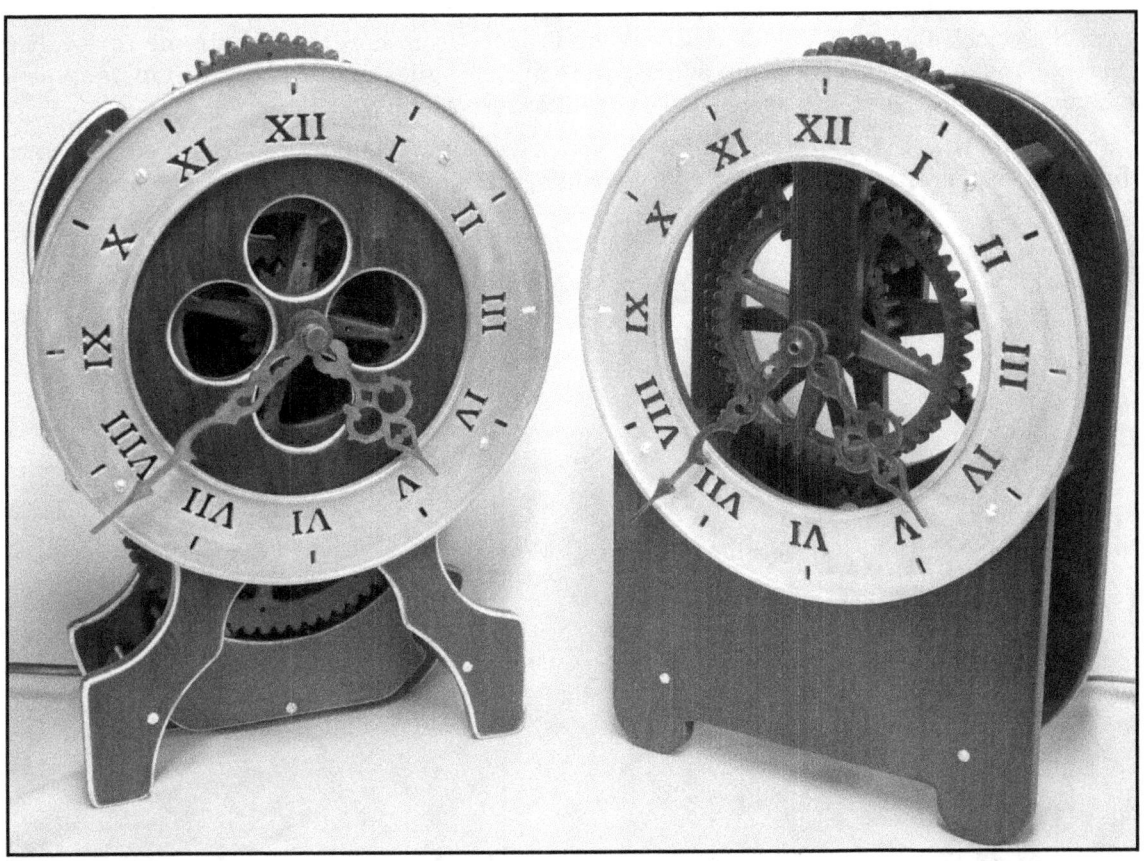

Whatever design you go with, it is important to take away one thing from this project: try new things.

The most difficult process in building an electric gear clock is the cutting of the gears. Once cut and finished you can use those gears in any clock based on the HANS design. This means you can experiment with the clock plates, face, and hands.

Note that the face can be removed by removing the hands and the top four mounting screws.

The clock shown in Figure 10.1 is the same clock, but by changing nothing but the shape of the clock plates you will get a drastically different clock. By changing the hands and the face you can change it even more. It is even possible to design the clock face directly into the front clock plate.

Throughout this book, MDF was used to make the clock plates. By using an exotic hardwood you can forgo the painting and simply apply a coat of shellac or polyurethane and create a different look.

As a rule the gears cannot be created from solid wood, but by cutting thin sheets of hardwood and gluing them up at right angles to each other, you can create some laminated stock that is suitable for the gears. The clock shown in Figure 10.2 was made 100% from hardwood. Extreme care was taken when cutting and assembling the gears as they were quite fragile, and in a couple of instances repairs had to be made when a gear was dropped. The results were worth the effort.

When you build the HANS electric gear clock, you are not just a building a clock. You are learning a clock building system that is limited only by your imagination.

Figure 10.1

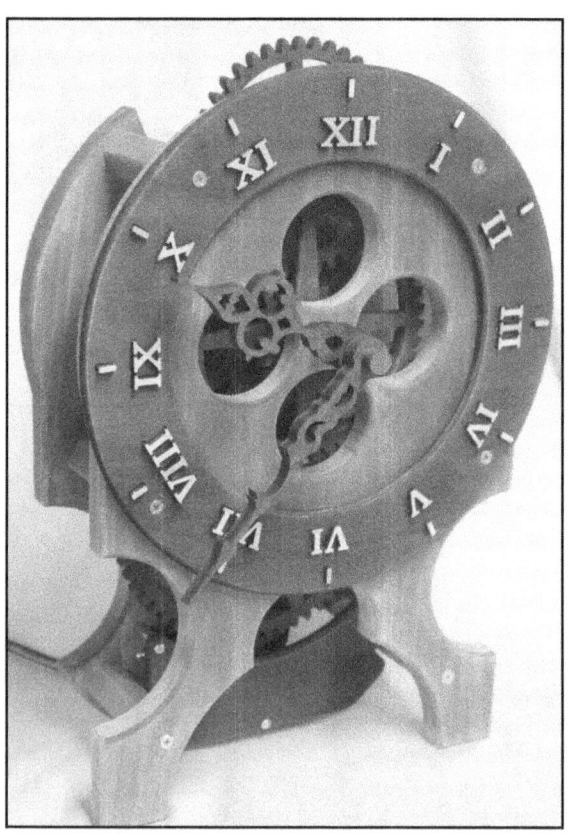

Figure 10.2

Appendix A

Drawings

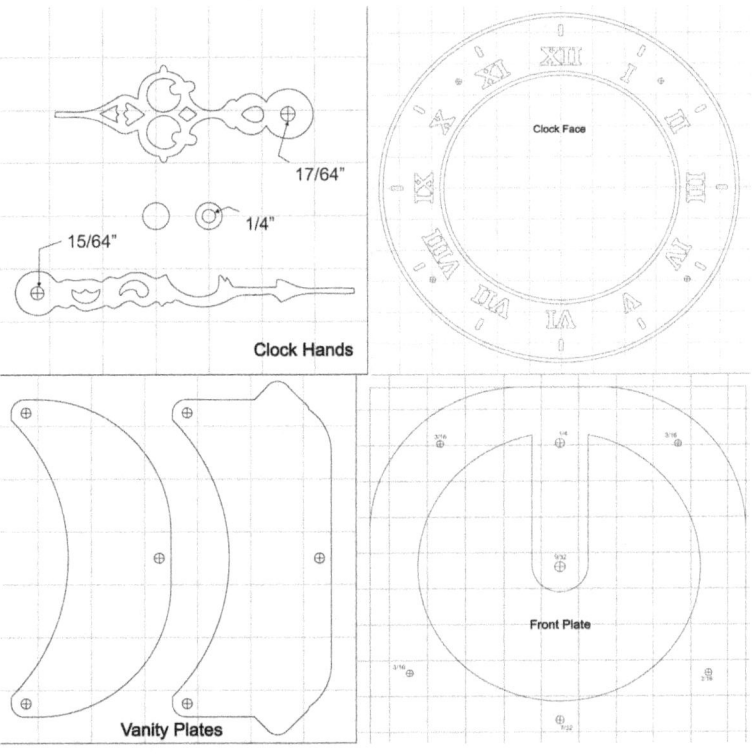

The drawings in this chapter are provided to help you in the completion of your clock regardless of how you create or acquire your final gears.

Many of the drawings are scaled down to fit the page. If you want to use them as templates for a scroll saw then you will need to copy and enlarge them. The actual drawings have been moved to the outside of the sheets to make copping easier.

The following table shows the percent of enlargement needed to obtain the full size drawing.

40% = 250%
70% = 143%
80% = 125%
90% = 111%

Clock Face

Outside diameter is 11-1/4". Inside diameter is 7-1/4".

The face is made from three pieces of 1/8" stock. The main face has an outside diameter of 11-1/4" and an inside diameter of 7-1/4". The outer ring has an outside diameter of 11-1/4" and an inside diameter of 11". The inner ring has an outside diameter of 7-1/2" and an inner diameter of 7-1/4".

The two rings are glued to the main face once the slits, holes, and numbers have been cut or marked. The four mounting holes are 3/16" in diameter.

Grid lines have been provided so that multiple sheets may be enlarged, cut, and taped together. Each grid is 1"x 1".

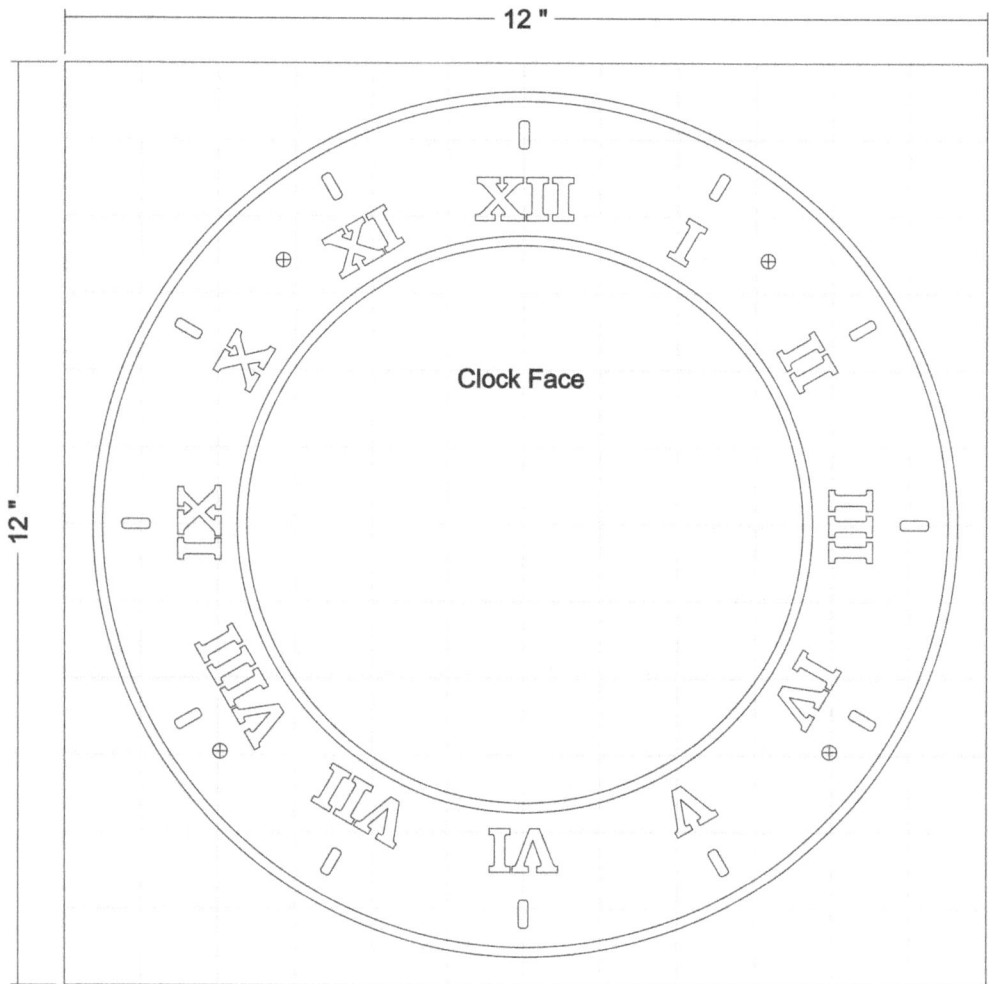

Scaled 40%

Front Plate

The front plate has a base shape of 10" x 15-1/4" and should be made from 1/2" stock. The stock can be any material, including hardwood. The three center holes are critical, as they hold the gears. All the other holes are for attaching the two plates. All the holes in the front plate should match the holes in the rear plate.

Grid lines have been provided so that multiple sheets may be enlarged, cut, and taped together. Each grid is 1"x 1".

The center cutout is 7.5" in diameter.

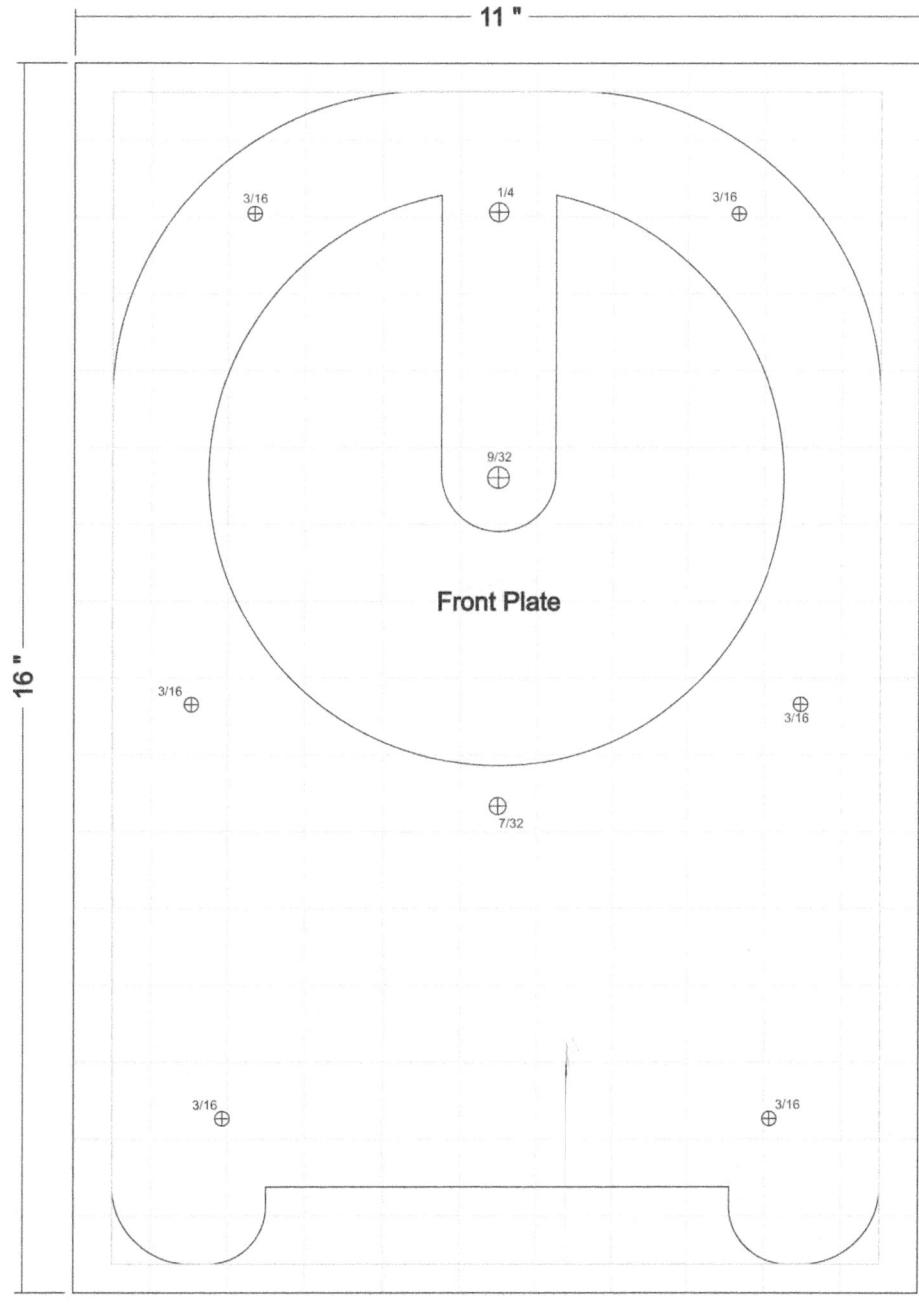

Scaled 40%

Building the Hans Electric Gear Clock

Rear Plate

The rear plate has a base shape of 10" x 15-1/4" and should be made from 1/2" stock. The stock can be any material, including hardwood. The two center holes are critical, as they hold the gears. All the other holes are for attaching the two plates. All the holes in the front plate should match the holes in the rear plate. Depending on the motor used, only one set of motor mounting holes need to be cut.

Grid lines have been provided so that multiple sheets may be enlarged, cut, and taped together. Each grid is 1"x 1".

The center cutout is 7.5" in diameter.

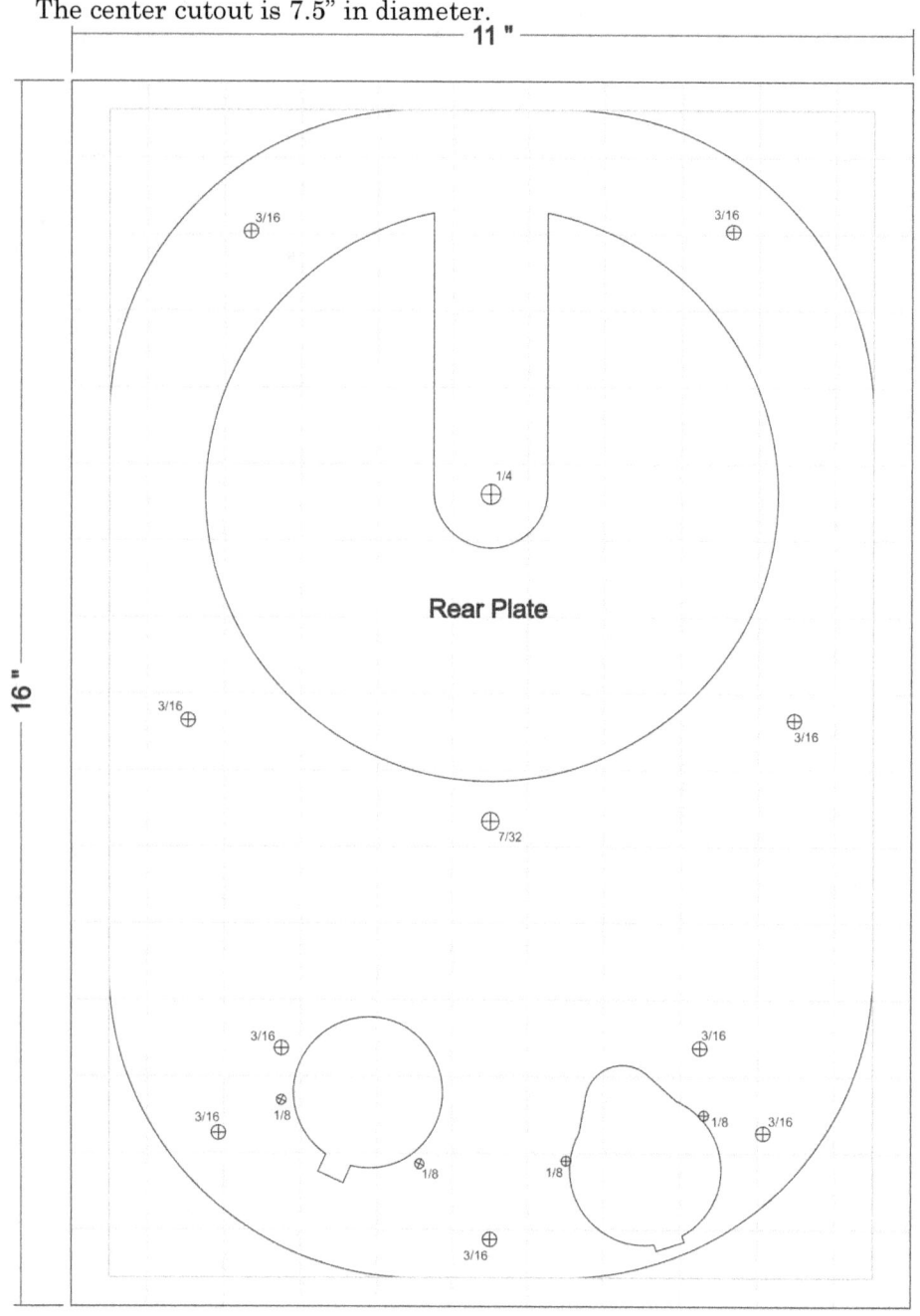

Scaled 40%

116   *Appendix A*   Drawings

Gear 3

60 tooth gear 7.29" in diameter with a 1/4" center hole.

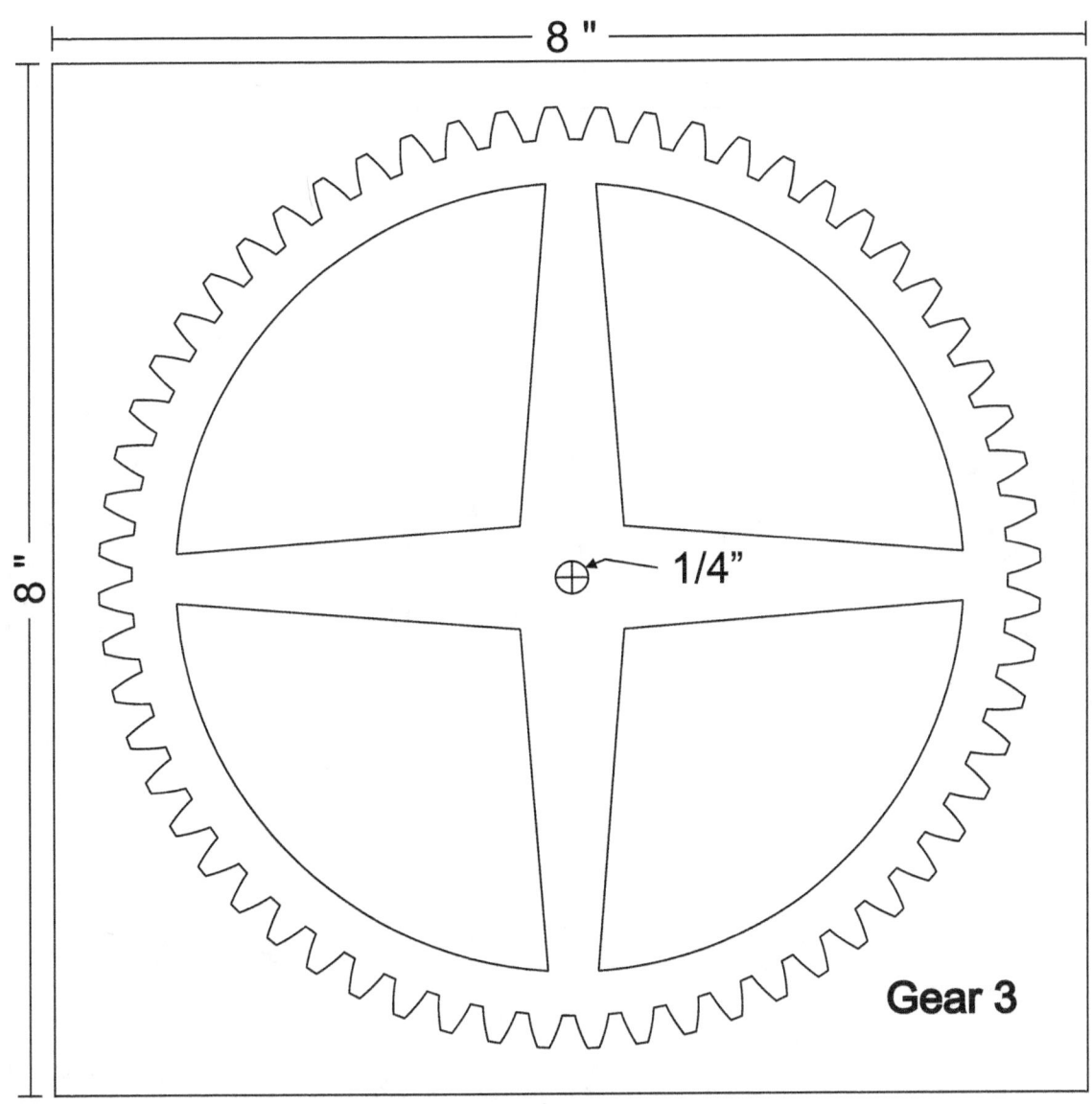

Scaled 70%

Building the Hans Electric Gear Clock

Gear 5

64 tooth gear 7.765" in diameter with a 1/4" center hole.

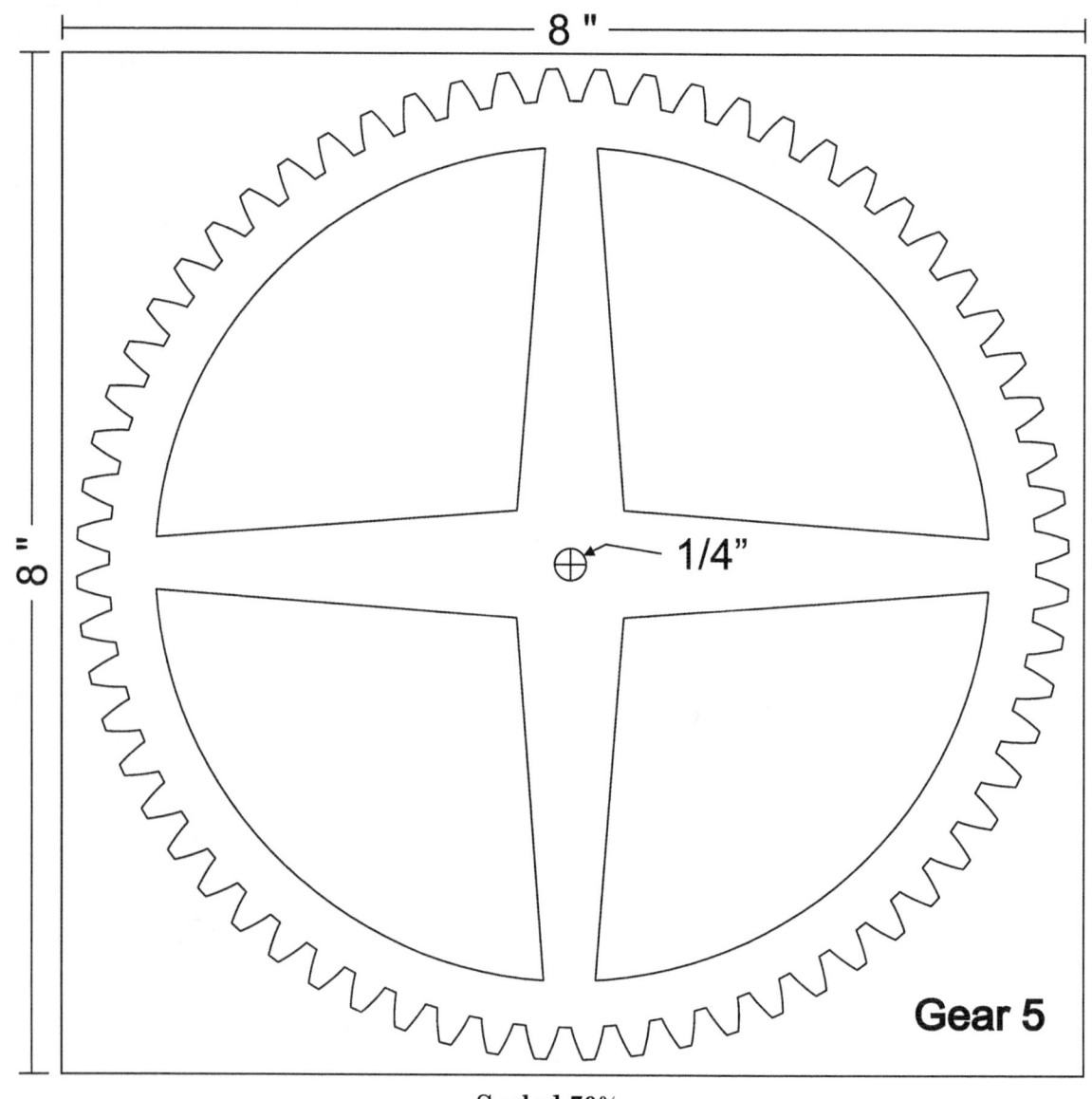

Gear 5

Scaled 70%

Gear 7

40 tooth gear 4.94" in diameter with a 9/32" center hole. This gear has a pocket that is 5/8" in diameter and .17" deep. The purpose of this pocket is to house a small locking washer 1/8" thick that will hold the gear on the arbor.

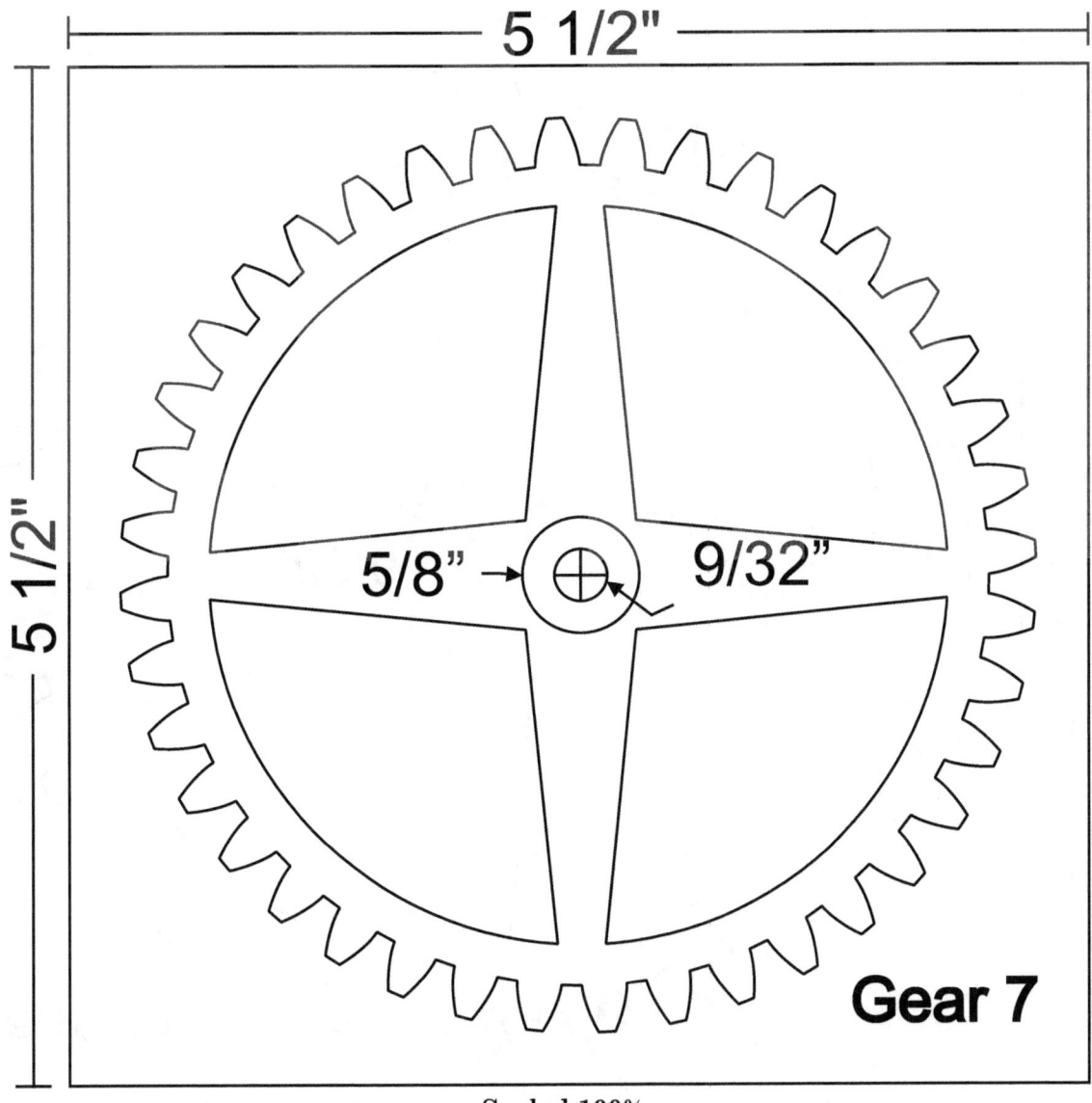

Scaled 100%

Building the Hans Electric Gear Clock

Gear 9

48 tooth gear 5.88" in diameter with a 9/32" center hole.

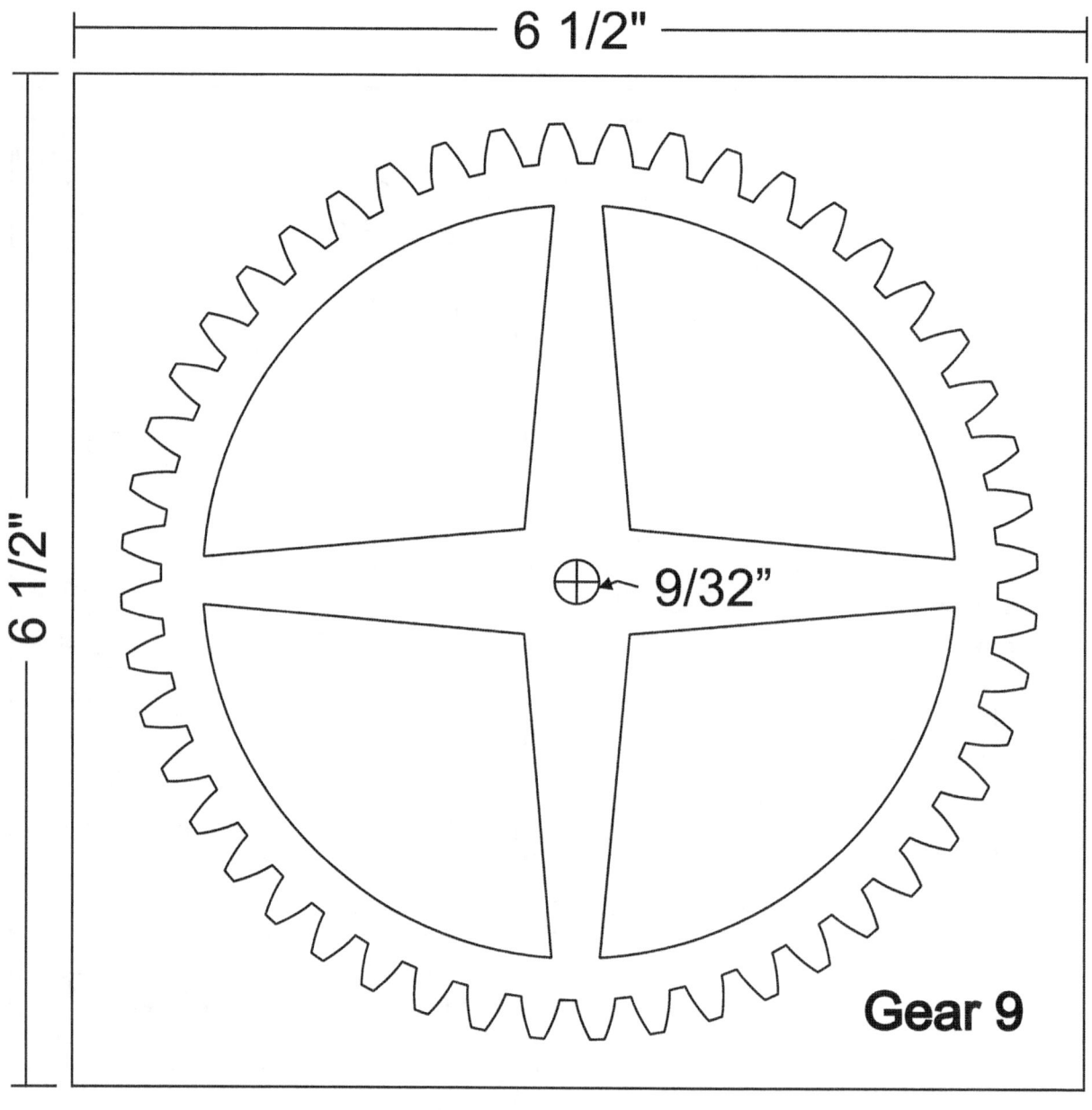

Scaled 90%

Small Gears

Gear 4 - 8 tooth gear, 1.8" in diameter with a 1/4" center hole.
Gear 6 - 16 tooth gear, 2.25" in diameter with a 1/4" center hole.
Gear 8 - 10 tooth gear, 1.41" in diameter with a 9/32" center hole.
Drive Gear - 8 tooth gear, 1.8" in diameter with a 3.16" center hole.

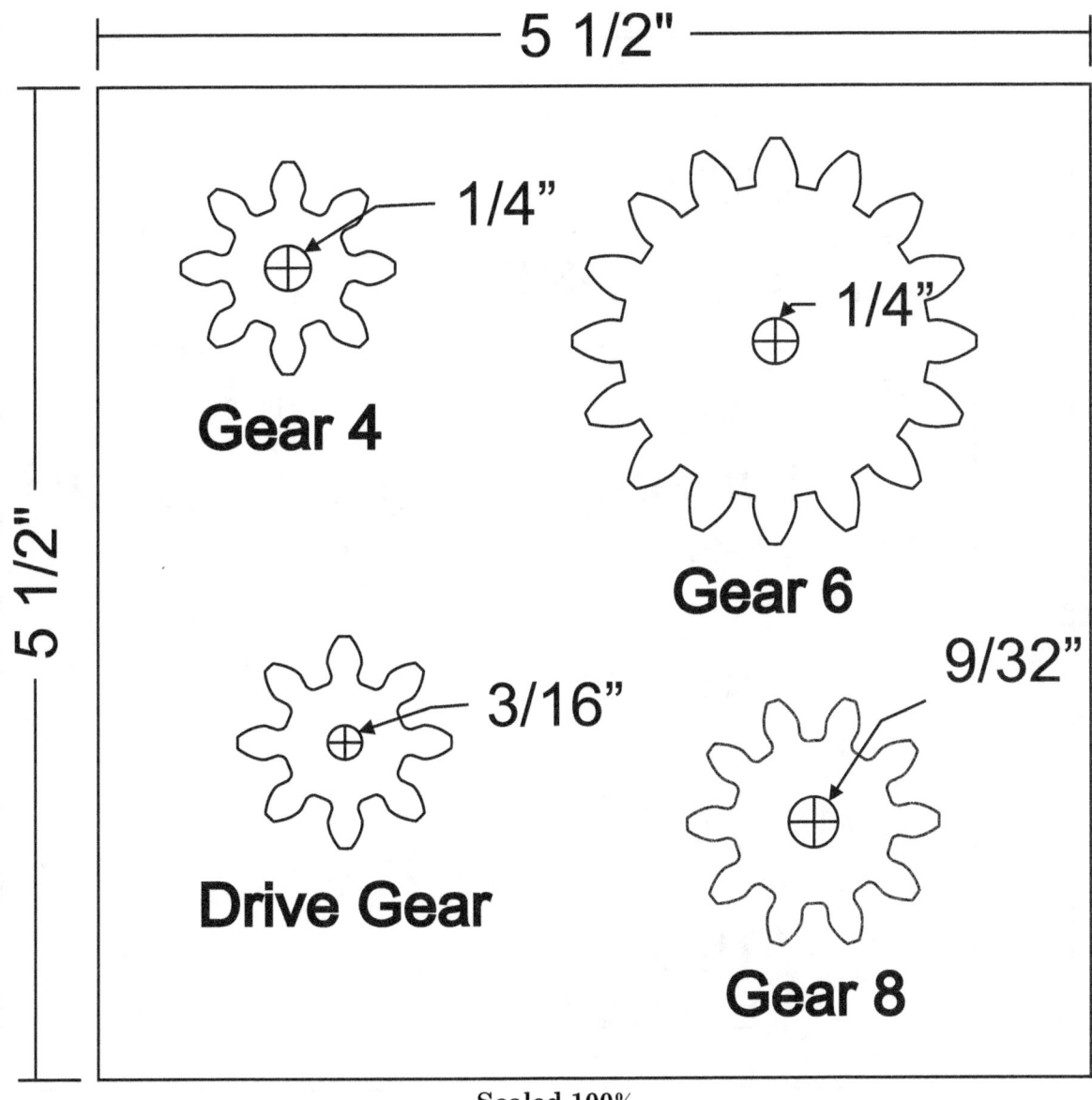

Scaled 100%

Building the Hans Electric Gear Clock

Thick Spacers

Thick Spacer 1 - 3/4" x 3/4" with a 7/32" center hole.
Thick Spacer 1 - 3/4" x 3/4" with a 7/32" center hole.
Thick Spacer 3 - 3/4" x 3/4" with a 1/4" center hole.

The extra holes are optional on the HANS electric gear clock. The thick spacers should be the same thickness as the gears. Normally, they should be made from the same stock.

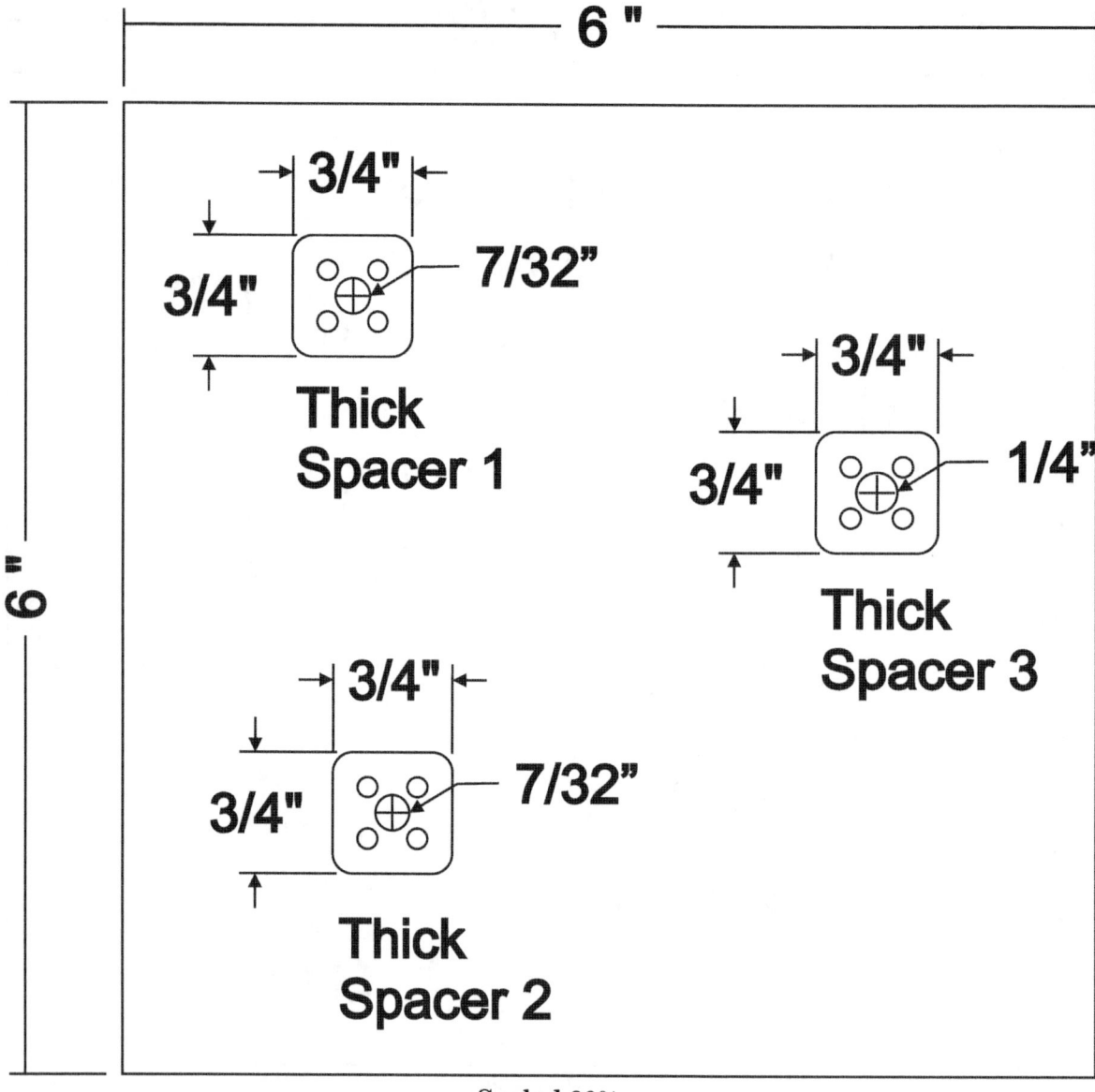

Scaled 90%

Gear Spacers

Gear Spacer 1 : 5/8" diameter with a 1/4" center hole.
Gear Spacer 2 : 1" diameter with a 1/4" center hole.
Gear Spacer 3 : 3/4" diameter with a 9/32" center hole.

The extra holes are optional on the HANS electric gear clock. The gear spacers are all 1/8" thick.

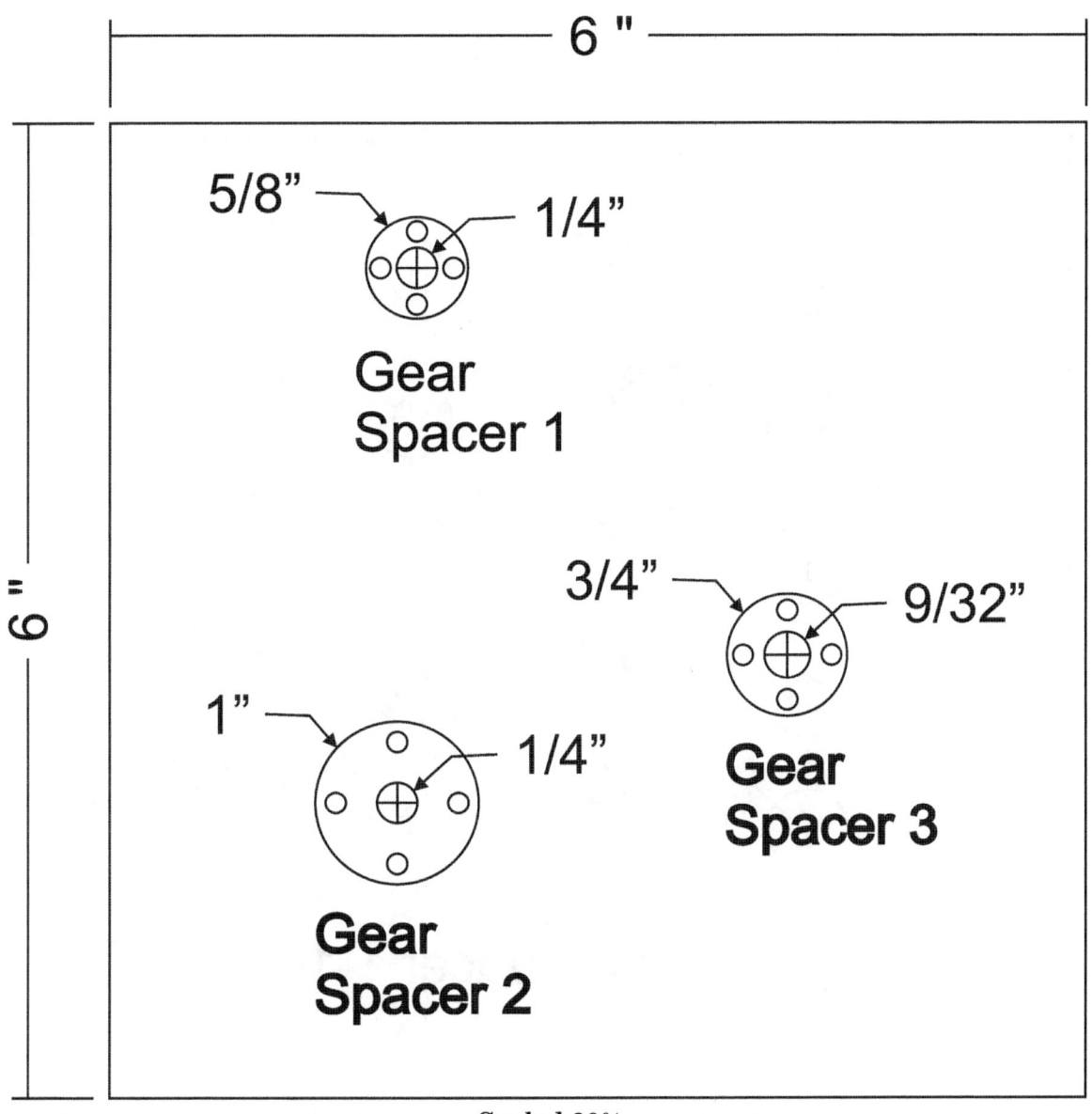

Scaled 90%

Thin Spacers 1-10

Thin Spacer 1-10 : 7/32" center hole.

The thin spacers are all 1/8" thick.

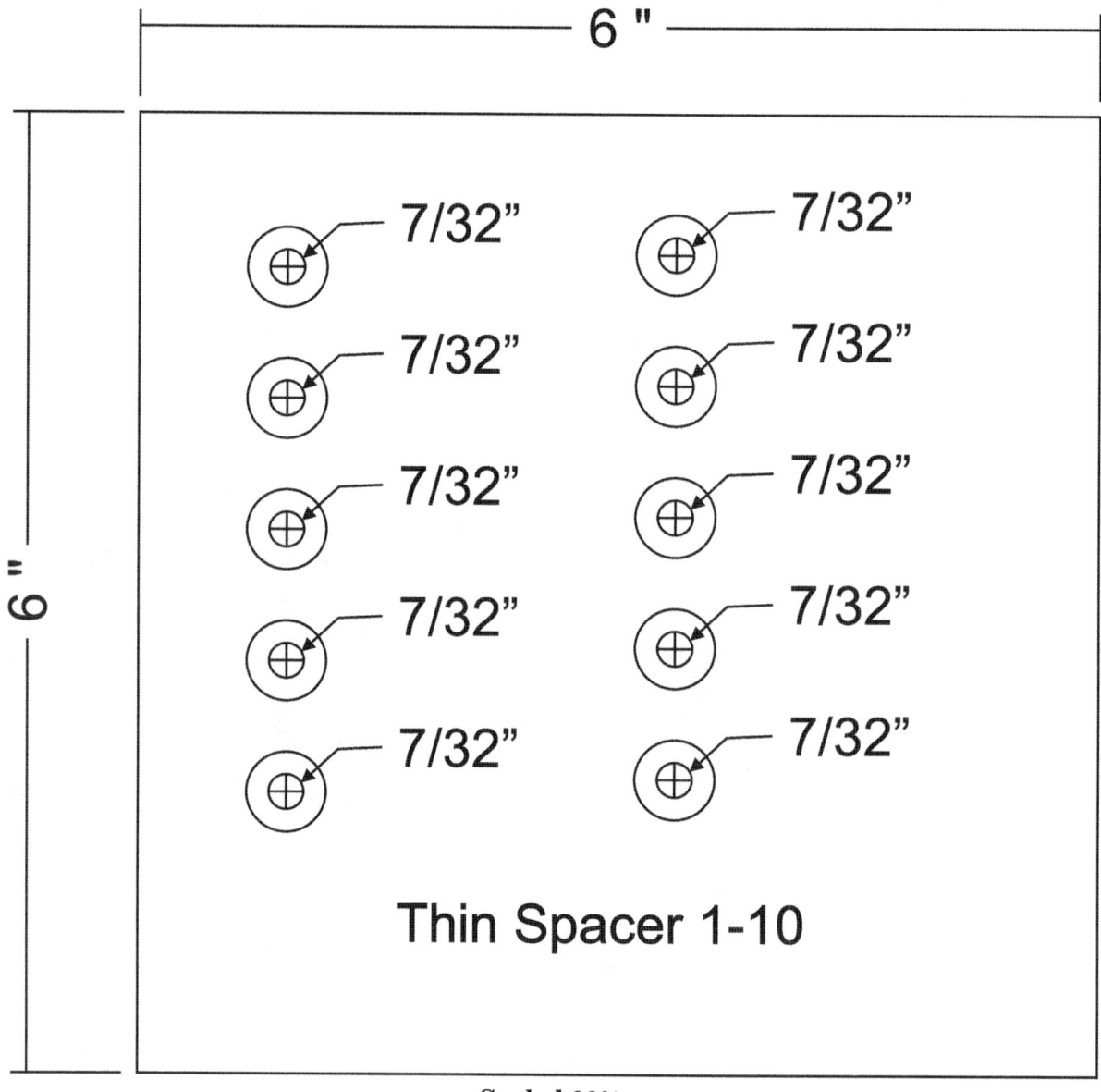

Scaled 90%

Thin Spacers 11-17

Thin Spacer 11-15 : 1/4" center hole.

Thin Spacer 16 : .24" center hole with relief slit (used to hold gear 7 in place).

Thin Spacer 17: 9/32" center hole.

The thin spacers are all 1/8" thick.

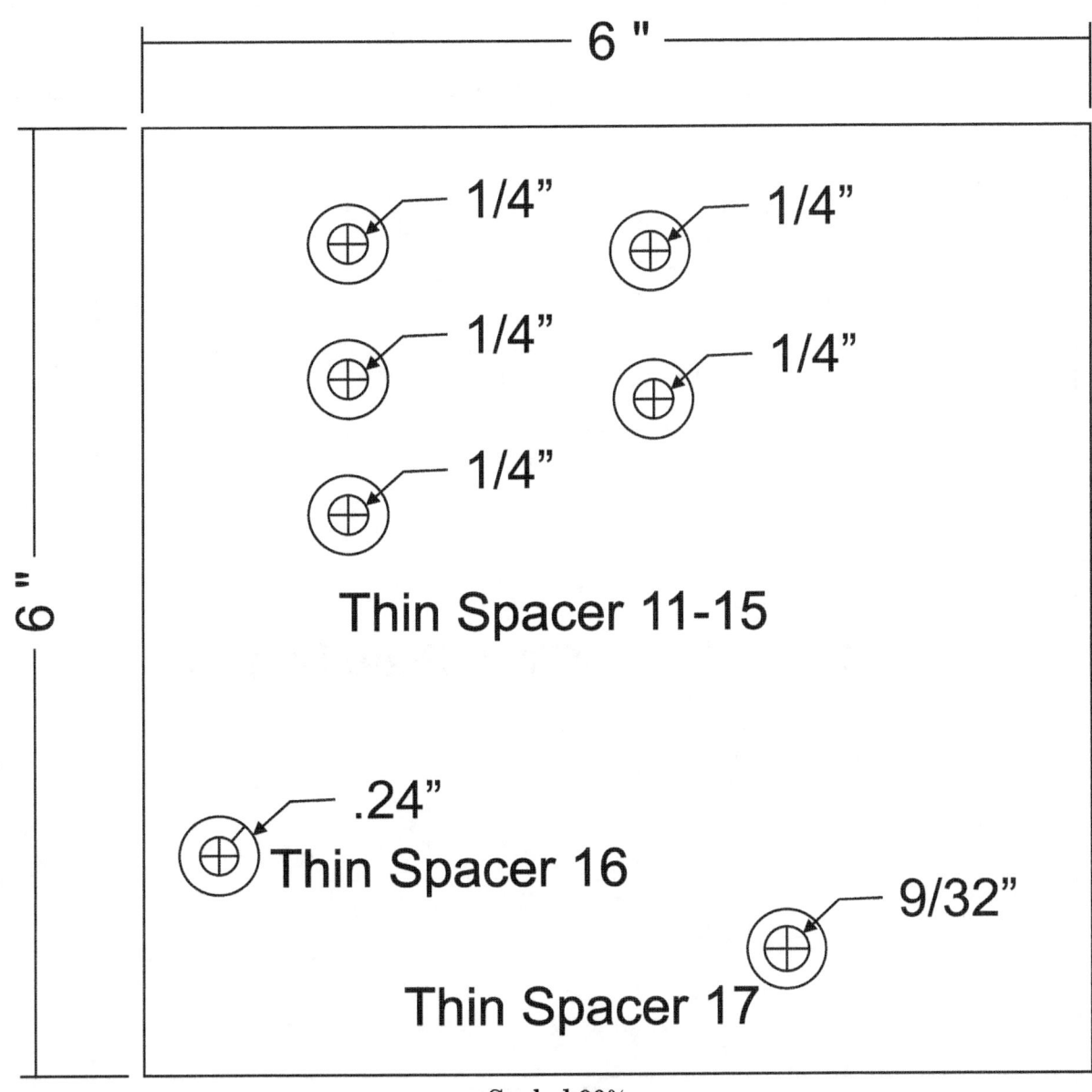

Scaled 90%

Clock Plate Spacers

1/2" x 1/2" x 2-3/4" piece of stock with a 1/8" pilot hole on each end that is 1" deep.

These can be made of any material and can be 1/2" x 1/2" to 3/4" x 3/4" thick

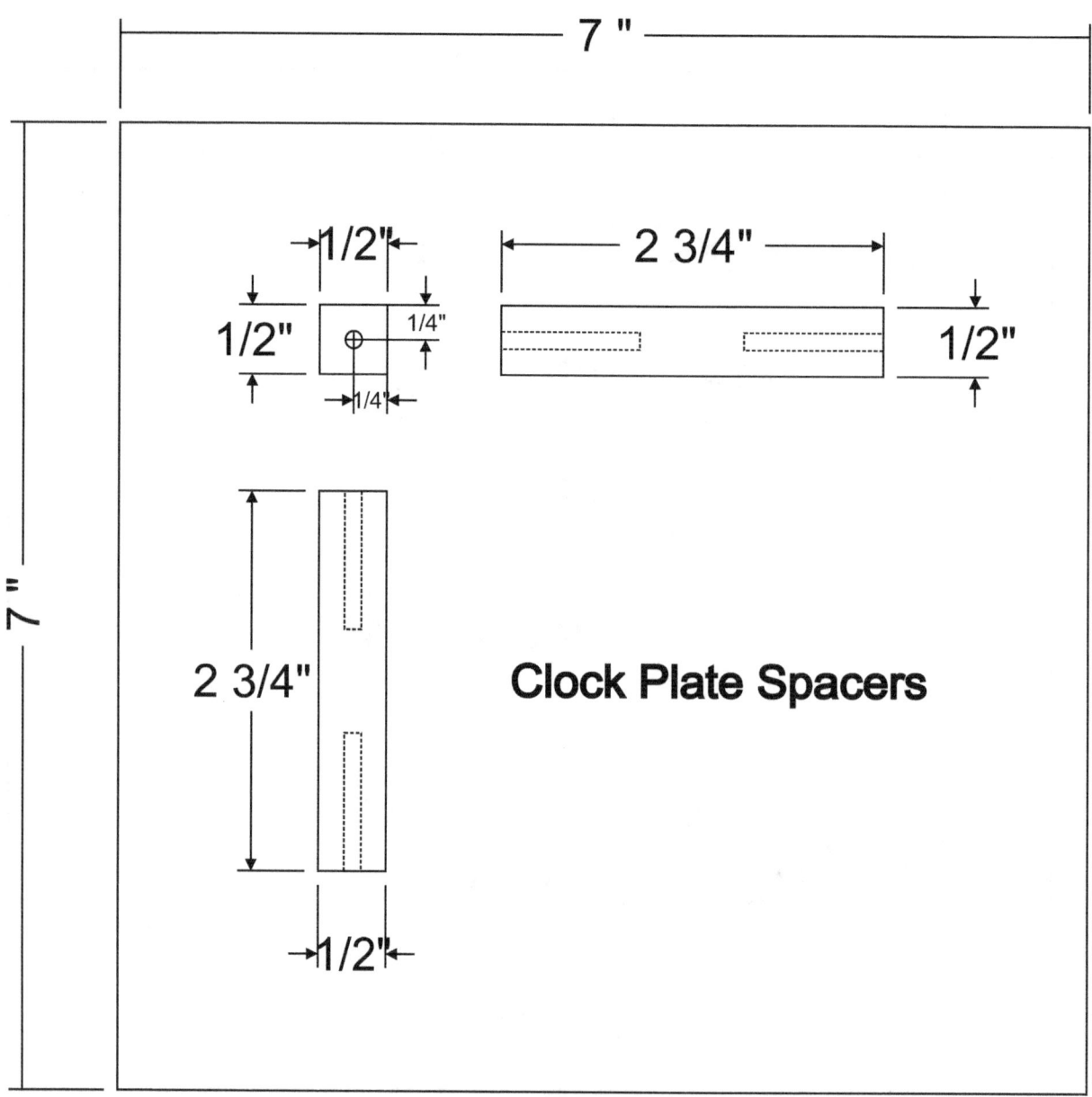

Vanity Plates

The vanity plates can be made from any stock and should be 1/8" thick. You can, however, increase the thickness but you will then need longer mounting screws.

All holes are 3/16" in diameter.

Note that the background squares are 1" x 1".

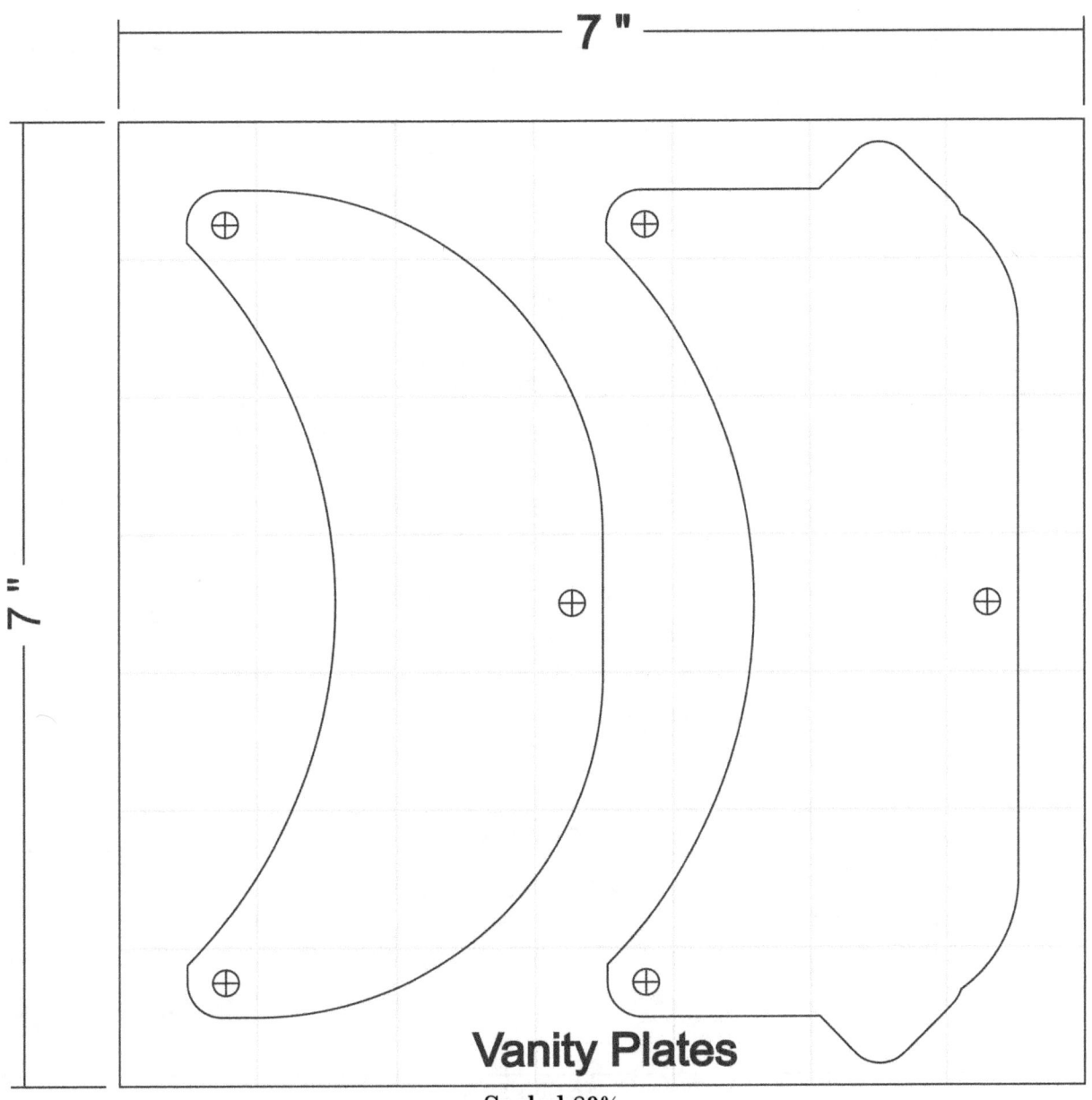

Vanity Plates
Scaled 80%

Building the Hans Electric Gear Clock

Clock Hands

Hour hand has 17/64" mounting hole.

Minute hand has 15/64" mounting hole.

Clock hands can be made from any material and can be up to 1/4" thick.

Note that the background squares are 1" x 1".

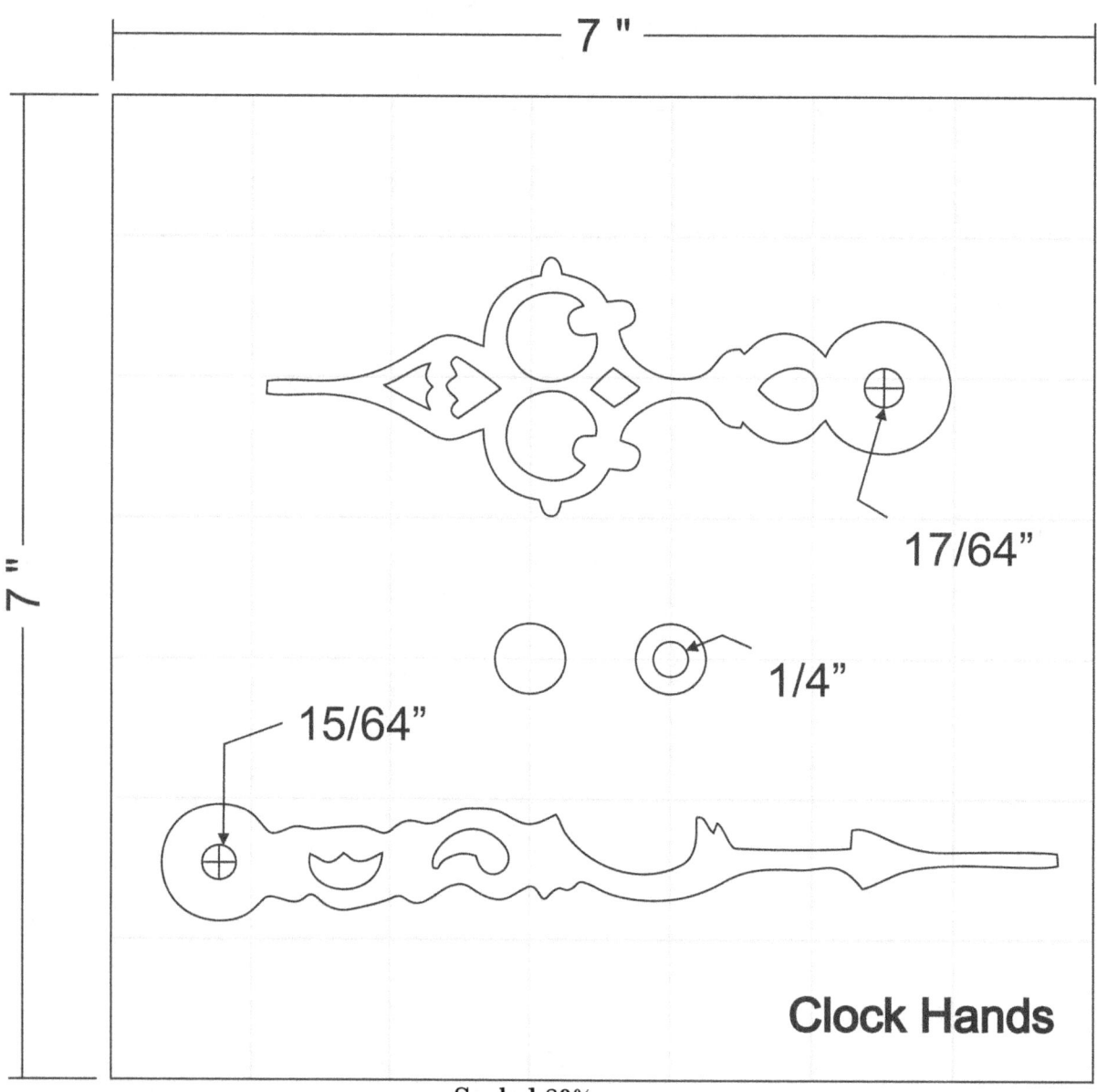

www.ingramcontent.com/pod-product-compliance
Lightning Source LLC
Chambersburg PA
CBHW082126230426
43671CB00015B/2816